RECENT UNITED STATES POLICY

IN THE PERSIAN GULF

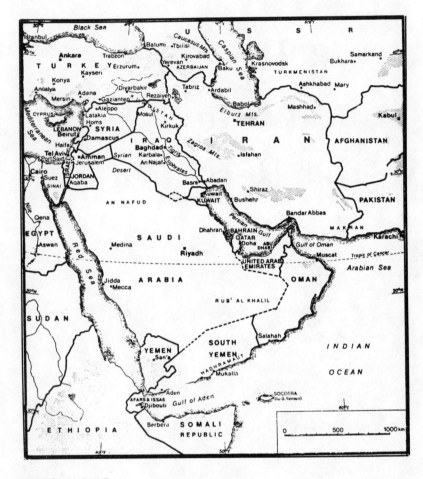

PERSIAN GULF
REGION

# Recent United States Policy in the Persian Gulf (1971-82)

C. Paul Bradley

Tompson & Rutter
Grantham, NH 03753

© *C. Paul Bradley 1982*

△

*Library of Congress Cataloging in Publication Data*

Bradley, C. Paul
Recent United States policy in the Persian Gulf
(1971-82)

Bibliography: p.
1. Persian Gulf Region--Foreign relations
--United States
2. United States--Foreign relations
--Persian Gulf Region.
I. Title
DS326.B7  1982        327.730536            82-16049
ISBN 0-936988-08-8  (pbk.)

△

First published 1982 by Tompson & Rutter Inc,
Grantham, New Hampshire, 03753-0297
and
distributed by The Shoe String Press Inc,
Box 4327, Hamden, Connecticut 06514

*Printed in the United States of America*

to Anna

*Author's Note*

This report is intended primarily for use by undergraduate students in courses on American foreign policy and the Middle East and for the general public. Certain documentary sources were made available to the author at the Libraries of the University of Michigan in Ann Arbor, Michigan.

The author has published two other monographs on the Middle East: *The Camp David Peace Process* and *Electoral Politics in Israel: The Knesset Election of 1981*. Both were published in 1981 by Tompson and Rutter, Grantham, N. H. Previously he has done field research in the Caribbean and Southeast Asia, and his findings are published in several scholarly journals. He presently teaches political science at the University of Michigan–Flint.

Grateful acknowledgment is made of valued editorial assistance by the author's wife, Anna.

# Contents

# Introduction

In the last decade American awareness and concern regarding the Persian Gulf region have significantly increased.(1)  It is now widely accepted that unimpeded access to Persian Gulf oil facilities is crucially important to the economic well-being, if not the survival of the United States and its allies in Western Europe and Japan.(2)  At the same time the Gulf is seen as an increasingly important cockpit of superpower rivalry between the U.S. and the Soviet Union, especially since the Soviet invasion of Afghanistan in late 1979. Some observers have argued that a future Soviet-American clash in the Persian Gulf may trigger off World War III.

*Two Phases in U.S. Policy in the Gulf*

The precipitant of the recently enlarged American interest in the Persian Gulf was the British withdrawal from Aden and the Gulf sheikdoms completed in 1971.(3)  For a quarter century in the East-West cold war Britain had been the primary guardian of Western security interests in the Gulf with the United States assuming a marginal supportive role.  Since 1971 there have been two major phases in the unfolding American involvement in the Gulf.  The first phase covered the period 1971-78 when Washington relied primarily on regional surrogates, armed with weapons supplied by the U.S. and instructed by U.S. military technicians.  Since collapse of the Pahlavi monarchy in Iran in 1979, the U.S. has stressed a unilateral buildup of its own military power in the region, hampered by the marked reluctance of most local states to enter into close military arrangements with Washington. In the second phase the major focus of U.S. strategic planning has been the controversial Rapid Deployment Force, heavily dependent on effective projection of U.S. air and sealift capabilities.  These successive phases of U.S. policy are the subject of this report.


*The Gulf Setting*

In the Persian Gulf American policymakers confront a region of great complexity.  Its constituent units are in differential stages of rapid modernization, manifest marked political instability, and are prey to a complex of intra-regional conflicts.  Three of the eight states in the Gulf proper require special attention:  Iran, Saudi Arabia, and Iraq, the three leading oil exporters in the Middle East.

*Iran*, the single non-Arab state in the region, is the most populous.  Its population of over 38 million is greater than that of the other seven

Gulf states combined. Boasting a high-level culture of ancient lineage, Iranians have habitually considered themselves superior to their Arab neighbors. The entire eastern littoral of the Persian Gulf is Iranian. Iran's long northern border with Russia has made it vulnerable both under the Tsar and the Soviet Communists. Under the ambitious military buildup sponsored by the late Shah, Mohammed Reza Pahlavi, and strongly supported by the United States, Iran was clearly the strongest military power in the Gulf. In the 1970s the Shah pursued a policy of Iranian hegemony in the Gulf, sometimes called *Pax Iranica*, which was projected beyond the Gulf to the Arabian and Indian oceans.

Iran adheres to the Twelver Shia sect of Islam (4), and under the present regime dominated by Ayatollah Khomeini, Iran has become the fount of revolutionary Islamic fundamentalism. Its present attraction for large Shia communities in Iraq, Saudi Arabia's Eastern Province, Bahrain, and other Gulf states may eventually lead to a more successful assertion of Iranian hegemony in the Gulf than the late Shah enjoyed. But few specialists are now willing to predict the outcome of the succession struggle which will inevitably follow the death of the aged Khomeini and its uncertain implications for Iran's primacy in the Gulf.

*Saudi Arabia*, with a much smaller population variously estimated at between 5 and 9 million, derives its increasing importance and prestige from its exceptionally large oil reserves; the great wealth it acquired as a result of the quadrupling of world oil prices in 1973-74; its special role as the custodian of the Muslim holy places in Mecca and Medina; and its leadership position among the "moderate" Arab states. The Kingdom of Saudi Arabia is the product of a prolonged military effort coupled with skillful diplomacy carried out by King

Abdul Aziz ibn Saud and completed in 1926. Its stability rests on the smooth functioning of a complex tribal network owing allegiance to the al-Sauds. Nearly all important power positions are held by Saudi princes, whose individual positions are based on rival factions within the royal family. The prevailing authoritarian character of the government is tempered by the long-established pattern of royal "consultations" in which private citizens petition for redress of grievances on an informal basis. The state religion upheld by the royal family is that of the puritanical Wahhabi sect of Sunni Muslims.

Private American oil companies played a pivotal role in the development of Saudi Arabia's rich oil resources, and even today the ARAMCO Company, although formally nationalized by the Saudi Government, is an extremely important element in the Saudi economy. In the 1970s, the Saudis, enriched by the sharp escalation in world oil prices, embarked on a massive program of economic and military modernization, which embodies an extremely rapid rate of social change. A special and potentially disruptive feature of the present Saudi economy is its heavy dependence on a largely foreign work force of between 1.5-2 million expatriates.(5) These include large numbers of Yemeni workers and Palestinian Arabs, the latter holding influential positions in all sectors. Speculation is widespread as to whether the traditional Saudi political order will prove sufficiently flexible to cope with such a rapidly changing social order.

Since the dramatic wartime meeting in 1945 of U.S. President Franklin Roosevelt and Ibn Saud on a warship in Egypt's Great Bitter Lake, the U.S. has formed a "special relationship" with Saudi Arabia. It is compounded of increasingly sophisticated weapon sales; an American community of military advisers and representatives of private firms engaged in the modernization program, presently estimated at 40,000; an expanding trade in U.S. goods and heavy Saudi investment of "petrodollars" in U.S. financial holdings. Saudi relations with both Iran and Iraq have been intermittently troubled. Since the fall of the pro-Western Shah in 1979 relations with stridently anti-Western Iran have seriously deteriorated. With substantial Saudi support for Iraq in its current war with Iran, Saudi relations with Iraq have considerably improved.

*Iraq* represents a formidable force of secular radicalism in the Gulf region. Since the fall of the pro-Western Hashimite dynasty in 1958, Iraq has pursued an aggressively revolutionary policy. After a coup in 1968 the Baath Party held uninterrupted control of the Iraqi government. The post-war Baath socialist movement was pan-Arab in its origins, but severe frictions developed between its Syrian and Iraqi branches. At certain intervals armed conflict between the two neighboring states appeared imminent.

Significantly in the Iraqi-Iran war Baathist Syria strongly supports Iran despite their ideological differences. Some Iraqi leaders fear Syria's President Assad is bent on the absorption of their Baath government, weakened by heavy war losses. In domestic policy the Iraqi government has been identified with land reform including some recourse to agricultural cooperatives and collectives, rapid industrialization, and a harshly repressive policy against its internal opponents.

Prior to the 1958 revolution Iraq was a bulwark of Western policy in the Middle East serving as linch-pin in the U.S.-sponsored Baghdad regional security pact. Under the Baath Iraq formed close relations with the Soviet Union, culminating in the 1972 Soviet-Iraqi Friendship Treaty. The Soviet Union became Iraq's principal arms supplier and source of technical assistance for economic development.

The Sunni-Shia religious divisions in Iraq are extremely important with the Shia majority being ruled by a political elite comprised mostly of Sunni Muslims. The fall of the Iranian Shah in 1979 and the subsequent internal turmoil in Iran emboldened Iraq's President Saddam Hussein to initiate war with Iran in the fall of 1980. Mixed motives were ascribed to President Hussein. Iraqi military action against Iran was partly seen as a preemptive strike to prevent the crossover of Shia fundamentalism into Iraq. A minimal war goal was to assure future Iraqi control over the long disputed Shatt al-Arab waterway at the mouth of the Gulf. Propaganda appeals were made to the Arab majority in Iranian Khuzistan. To other Gulf states Iraq was seen as bent on regional hegemony.

In the Arab-Israel conflict Iraq has been an intransigent "hard-liner" state opposing Israel. After Sadat indicated his willingness in 1977 to make formal peace with the despised Israel, Iraq played a leading role in a collective Arab effort to isolate Egypt. Baathist Iraq has had intermittently troubled relations with the Gulf's conservative sheikdoms. Iraq's territorial claims on Kuwait have several times led to serious border clashes. With the recent cooling in Soviet-Iraq relations U.S. relations with Iraq have improved, although full diplomatic relations broken in 1967 have not been renewed.

The smaller Gulf sheikdoms have since 1971 received uneven attention from U.S. policymakers. Oil-rich *Kuwait*, independent since 1961 and the only conservative sheikdom to maintain diplomatic relations with the Soviet Union, has been the recipient of a relatively modest program of U.S. arms sales since 1973. The ancient *Sultanate of Oman*

14

occupies a pivotal strategic position in the Gulf overlooking the vitally important "choke point" at the Strait of Hormuz through which Gulf oil tankers must pass as they move into the Arabian Sea. In the mid-1970s this traditional sultanate was enabled with the aid of foreign troops supplied by the Shah of Iran to suppress a Soviet-supported leftist rebellion in Dhofar Province, bordering on radical Marxist South Yemen. Oman's modernizing Sultan, Qabus bin Said, was the only Arab Gulf state to support the 1979 Egyptian-Israeli peace treaty. Subsequent to the Soviet invasion of Afghanistan in 1979 Oman has been the only Gulf state signing a military "access agreement" with the United States which permits limited U.S. use of Omani facilities in a future Gulf crisis.

*Bahrain* has been chiefly important to the U.S. in providing certain port facilities for the small U.S. naval unit in the Gulf, known as MIDEASTFOR. This arrangement was originally made under the aegis of the British in 1949 and reaffirmed when Bahrain became independent in 1971. But escalating Arab nationalism after the 1973 war with Israel led Bahrain to restrict Western use of these facilities. The ruling al-Khalifa family, who are Sunni Muslims, is confronted with an increasingly restive Shia population. The Shias constitute a majority of about 60 percent of the population and are subject to influence by Islamic revolutionaries in Iran. In December 1981 the conservative Gulf states were greatly agitated by an abortive coup attempt by Bahraini Shias which the Bahraini government claimed Iran had instigated. In the aftermath Saudi Arabia and Bahrain concluded a mutual security agreement.

U.S. relations with the other two Gulf states, the *United Arab Emirates* (UAE), and the small sheikdom of *Qatar*, are accorded a relatively low priority. The UAE, a loose federation of seven

emirates formed in 1971, is the fifth largest in
the Middle East. Its relatively small population
of 900,000 enjoys one of the highest per capita in-
comes in the world. The UAE's federal government
has been riven by rivalry between the rulers of its
two most important units, Abu Dhabi and Dubai. With
an Iranian population of a hundred thousand, Dubai
is subject to special pressure from revolutionary
Iran whose Ayatollah Khomeini visited Dubai in May,
1979. In Qatar only 60,000 of the population of
about a quarter million are Qataris. The largest
of its heterogenous expatriate labor force are 50-
70,000 Pakistanis, 30-40,000 Iranians and 20,000
Palestinians. Qatar faces a decline in oil production in the late 1980s, and exhaustion of its
oil holdings is predicted after the year 2000. Both
the UAE and Qatar hold strongly anti-Communist
views that typify the conservative Gulf states. In
1975 the U.S. initiated a small-scale program of
arms sales to the UAE.


*The Two Yemeni States*

     At the southwestern corner of the Arabian pen-
insula North and South Yemen hold strategically
pivotal positions adjacent to the Strait of Bab al-
Mandeb lying between the Arabian and the Red Seas.
The People's Democratic Republic in South Yemen
(PDRY) is the single radical Marxist state in the
larger Gulf region. Due to its close relations
with the Soviet bloc the PDRY is widely viewed as
a major spearhead of expanding Soviet influence
in the Gulf. In the early 1970s South Yemen provided a sanctuary and important supply base for
leftist rebels in Oman's Dhofar Province. The
South Yemen armed forces employ a large contingent
of Soviet, East German, and Cuban military advisers.
(6) The ultimate outcome of the intermittent mer-

ger talks between radical South Yemen and the more conservative Yemen Arab Republic(YAR) in the north is problematic. Should an effective merger eventually be arranged and South Yemen's radical National Liberation Front(NLF) becomes the dominant political force in an integrated Yemen, a significant increase in Soviet bloc influence will follow.

Recent American involvement on behalf of North Yemen in its border disputes with South Yemen has been largely a function of the U.S. "special relationship" with Saudi Arabia. The U.S. shares Saudi fears of political radicalization in North Yemen. In early 1979 during the short border war between the two Yemens Saudi Arabia considered direct military intervention. Under Saudi prodding the Carter administration abruptly adopted a policy of emergency arms shipments and military advisers for North Yemen. With the cessation of hostilities there was a subsidence in Saudi and American interests. The YAR has demonstrated considerable skill in playing off the two superpowers against each other and has been the recipient of significant amounts of both Soviet and U.S. military and technical assistance. At present the YAR government is engaged in a bitter power struggle verging on civil war with its radical internal opposition, based in Aden. Should the latter prevail, merger of the two Yemens would probably follow without direct PDRY intervention.


*Larger Perspectives of U.S. Policymakers*

Due to the global character of Soviet-American rivalry, certain relevant geopolitical considerations, and the still unresolved Arab-Israeli conflict, U.S. officials concerned with Gulf policy must look beyond the Gulf itself. The larger geopolitical context includes the adjacent Arabian

Sea, the vast area covered by the Indian Ocean and
its littoral states and the politically turbulent
states in the Horn of Africa, Somalia, and Ethiopia, entry points to the Red Sea and Suez Canal.
These are the vital sea lanes which Persian Gulf
oil tankers regularly ply as well as Soviet and
U.S. naval fleets. The quickened interest of the
two superpowers in having assured access and available installations in the Indian Ocean coincided
with the 1968 announcement of the British withdrawal "east of Suez." With the evident reluctance of
Gulf states to grant the U.S. military bases, the
communications and logistical facilities made
available to the U.S. Navy in the British-owned
island of Diego Garcia in the Indian Ocean, have
acquired special importance.(7) Without Diego Garcia it is unlikely the U.S. could mount an effective military operation that a future Gulf crisis
might provoke.

The question of linkage between a settlement
of the long-standing Arab-Israeli dispute and a
strengthened Western position in the Persian Gulf
is much debated. Some observers argue that as long
as the United States fails to persuade Israel to
accept at least a partial withdrawal from the occupied territories in the West Bank and Gaza and
grant the Palestinian Arabs self-determination,
Washington cannot expect full Arab cooperation in
bolstering the presently precarious Western position in the Persian Gulf. Admittedly Kissinger's
"shuttle diplomacy" following the 1973 Arab-Israeli
war led to limited disengagement agreements between
Israel and two Arab states, Egypt and Syria. These
were followed by the 1979 Egyptian-Israeli Treaty
under the aegis of the Carter Administration, which
led to a complete Israeli withdrawal from Egyptian
Sinai in 1982. But for most Arabs this American-
sponsored peace process is regarded as woefully in-
adequate. In their eyes out-right Israeli annexa-

tion of the West Bank is a more likely prospect than the transitional Palestinian autonomy envisioned under the 1978 Camp David agreement. Critics of the linkage approach argue that even if the grievous Palestinian question were resolved to Arab satisfaction, effective U.S.-Arab collaboration in defense of the Gulf would not be assured. To these critics the formidable force of essentially anti-Western Arab nationalism and the prospective spread of virulently anti-Western Islamic fundamentalism are both inimical to Western goals and influence in the Gulf.

*Assessing Soviet Intentions
and Policies in the Gulf*

In the postwar decades two opposing views of Soviet global intentions and the appropriate U.S. response have confronted U.S. policy-makers. One view holds that the Soviet Union is inherently expansionist, operates in accordance with a master plan of external conquest and subversion, seeks the ultimate elimination of all Western zones of influence in contested areas, and ruthlessly exploits opportunities for Soviet advances which result from Western weakness. The upholders of this view advocate primary reliance on U.S. military power supported by its allies to either deter or defeat recurrent threats of Soviet expansion and the forging of mutual security arrangements with potential targets of Soviet aggression in contested areas. The feasibility of negotiating credible agreements with the Soviets is discounted, and occasional periods of relaxation in superpower tensions are regarded as highly transient.

The second school stresses the ascendant importance of the Soviet Union's status aspirations over its acknowledged power drives.(8) The governing assumption of this school is that if Western powers especially the U.S. granted the USSR wider participation in global decision-making, mutually beneficial accommodations would follow, and international tensions would be significantly lessened. In this view the virtual exclusion of the Soviet Union from the U.S.-sponsored peace process in the Middle East in both the Nixon and Carter administrations stimulated compensatory Soviet moves in Angola and the Horn of Africa. It is argued that the U.S. should deemphasize its military approach in contested areas, rely primarily on low-key diplomatic contacts to facilitate friendly relations with a wide range of Third World governments, and gradually build up a limited system of co-management of destabilizing regional disputes with the Soviet Union.

Among U.S. policymakers these opposing interpretations have been unevenly supported since 1947 with the pessimistic view of Soviet behavior usually having the greater number of adherents. In some administrations key officials embrace opposing views on this question as did Presidential adviser Brzezinski and Secretary of State Vance in the Carter administration, and the resultant acrimony adversely affects the coherence of U.S. policy. Certainly since 1979 the harsher view of the Soviets as irretrievably expansionist has prevailed in Washington.

Whatever the Russians' underlying motivations recent Soviet policy in the Persian Gulf has been pragmatic, flexible, and generally cautious in avoiding confrontation with Western powers. The invasion of Afghanistan in 1979 under special circumstances provides a contrasting exception. The principal Soviet objective in the Gulf region has been to reduce American influence and undermine the current predominance of the conservative states. Soviet relations have been predictably closer with

Baathist Iraq and Marxist South Yemen than with Saudi Arabia and the Gulf sheikdoms, where the USSR has diplomatic relations only with Kuwait.

The Soviets have utilized parallel devices in Iraq and South Yemen: very substantial arms sales and assignment of Soviet military advisers; technical assistance and support for development projects--a noteworthy example being Soviet aid in operation of the rich Rumaylah oil fields in northern Iraq; and the signing of treaties of friendship and cooperation--with Iraq in 1972 and the PDRY in 1979, which provided for close consultation between the signatories in emergency situations. In return Soviet Navy warships have periodically visited the Iraqi port of Umm Qasr--the Russians deny it constitutes a base, and in Aden the Soviets have access to important port and airfield facilities.

The Russians have also been involved at certain times in the internal policies of their two allies, supporting participation of the Iraqi Communists in the Baathist National Front and weighing in on the side of the more pro-Soviet faction in internal power struggles in the PDRY's ruling party. But in neither case does the Soviet Union escape periods of tension with its clients. This was especially true of Soviet-Iraqi relations in 1978 when the Communist Party attempt to infiltrate the Iraqi armed forces led to the execution of 21 Iraqi Communists.(9) The Soviet's regional position was further strengthened in 1981 when three pro-Soviet states--South Yemen, Ethiopia, and Libya formed a trilateral alliance, indicating the wider geopolitical context of Soviet policy in the Gulf.

As in other Third World areas Soviet policy is not confined to state-to-state relations with Gulf governments. In the early 1970s the Russians gave important support to the national liberation movement in Oman. When the Sultan's son, Qabus,

21

came to power by means of a coup in 1970, the Soviets charged it was a British-instigated "imperialist plot." Several delegations from the PDRY-based Popular Front for the Liberation of Oman and the Arabian Gulf(PFLOAG) were received in Moscow, and the Soviets reportedly gave important moral and material support to the 10-year rebellion which PFLOAG sustained in Dhofar province.(10)

The element of flexibility attributed to the Soviet Union's Gulf policy is illustrated in the surprisingly close relations established with pro-Western Iran in the 1960s. The turning point came in September 1962 when the Soviet Union accepted Iran's pledge that it would not permit foreign missile bases in its territory. Technological advances in intercontinental ballistics missiles had already reduced the threat of lesser missile sites in states on the Soviet periphery. Rapprochement with the Soviet Union enabled the Shah to reduce Iran's dependency on the United States without, however, jeopardizing his close relations with Washington. Over the next decade the Soviets became an important supplementary arms supplier to Iran. In 1965 the Shah visited Moscow and reached agreement on Soviet technical and financial assistance in building an iron and steel complex in Isfahan, a machine factory plant, and a gas pipeline to Soviet territory. Iran was to repay the USSR in natural gas and certain agricultural and industrial goods.(11) The Soviets supplied credits for the pipeline construction. Soviet exports to Iran increased tenfold, and by 1970 the USSR had become Iran's largest customer for non-oil exports. In this period Iran effectively used the threat of turning to Moscow, if the U.S. failed to meet Iran's intermittent requests for increased arms shipments.

Most regional specialists argue that the already extensive Soviet interests in the Persian Gulf will be greatly expanded as the Russians' own oil reserves are diminished over the next decade. Thus far the specialists have not reached consensus on either the exact timing of this significant shift or the degree of ultimate Soviet dependency on Gulf oil imports. But as future Gulf imports to the USSR increase, Soviet efforts either radically to curtail or even virtually shut off Gulf oil exports to the West and Japan are widely predicted in Western capitals.

*Summary of Regional Imperatives*

Certain distinguishing features which mark the Persian Gulf as an especially dynamic and volatile region require brief summation here. These are as follows:

(1) The central importance of oil as the key regional resource: oil as the major regional export and link to the industrial capitalist world of the West and Japan; the chief source of Government revenues in oil-producing countries, making possible the launching of multifaceted development projects; the source of suddenly acquired influence in world political councils and as a powerful weapon in inducing oil-consuming countries to support political preferences of the oil producers.

(2) The transitional character of most Gulf regimes: highly traditional societies whose cultural mores are undergoing rapid "modernization" in the Western sense; authoritarian political rule by tribally based ruling families, whose leaders are accustomed to deferential acquiesence by their subject populations and are fearful of participatory innova-

tions in their political systems; the steadily increasing number in the younger generations who are exposed to Western values and technology in their overseas studies.

(3) Significant imbalances in the populations of some Gulf states as in Kuwait, Qatar, and Abu Dhabi with the expatriate labor force, deprived of full citizenship privileges, outnumbering the local indigenous population. Many observers predict that the present pattern of their political non-involvement is unlikely to persist. In this diverse grouping the large number of well-educated expatriate Palestinian Arabs hold a special position as monitors of the anti-Israeli sentiments of their host governments.

(4) The dramatic regional impact of the recent wave of Islamic fundamentalism, rooted in a profound rejection of Western materialism and secular values, which emanates from Iran throughout the region. Its subversive appeal to the underprivileged and frequently impoverished Shia communities in the Gulf has not yet been fully tested. Its future spread may jeopardize the completion of the imported development projects favored by the rich oil-producer states.

(5) The visible tendency toward non-alignment in regional foreign policies. Even though particular states can be classified as either pro-Western or pro-Soviet, these orientations are subject to fluctuation and even reversal. In pressing their claims on one of the two competing superpowers Gulf states may main-

tain variable degrees of contact with the opposing camp. North Yemen accepts Soviet bloc aid, Saudi Arabia at times signals it may do so.

(6) The heavy reliance of the two competing superpowers on multimillion dollar arms sales as their major instrument of regional influence. The mutual reluctance of the Soviet Union and the U.S. to agree on limitations of either the quantity or level of sophistication of these imported weapons exacerbates the already high level of intra-regional tensions.

(7) The seemingly inherent instability of the regional balance of power as between the bloc of conservative states led by Saudi Arabia and those states who from markedly different stances challenge the regional status quo: Baathist Iraq, revolutionary Iran, and radical South Yemen. Significant shifts in the power balance can follow the overthrow of an established government as in Iran, the prolongation of an internal rebellion as in Oman, defeat for one side in a regional war as in the present Iranian-Iraq war, the resolution of a factional power struggle within a single ruling elite as in South Yemen. As a further complication the regional power balance is sensitive to changes in the relative power positions of the two superpowers as reflected in the nervous regional responses to the 1979 Soviet invasion of Afghanistan.

# I
## THE U.S. TWO-PILLAR POLICY
### IN THE GULF
### (1971-76)


*The Gulf and the Nixon Doctrine*

The 1968 announcement of Britain's imminent departure from the Persian Gulf coincided
with a dramatic drop-off in U.S. domestic support for its Vietnam war and the adoption of a
new U.S. policy of drastic retrenchment in its
overseas commitments. Even before the advent
of the Nixon administration in 1969 State Department officials made it clear the U.S. had
no intention of taking over British responsibilities in the Gulf. While the U.S. would
continue to be helpful to friendly states, local leaders in the region were expected to bear
the primary burden of regional defense.(12)
Full awareness of the American intent came
with the enunciation of the Nixon Doctrine in
June 1969. A basic differential was established
in future overseas responsibilities of the U.S.
For U.S. allies and states whose survival was

deemed vital to its national security the U.S.
promised to provide a nuclear shield from attack
by "a nuclear power." In cases of lesser aggression such states would bear "primary responsibility" for providing manpower for their own defense.
In these circumstances U.S. involvement would be
restricted to supplying military and economic assistance.(13)    Thus the United States would avoid
a precipitous retreat into isolationism, but at
the same time reduce direct U.S. military involvement abroad.

    Gradually U.S. policy in the Persian Gulf was
fitted into the framework of the Nixon Doctrine.
In 1973 two definitive statements of the full range
of U.S. interests in the Gulf were made in Congressional hearings.  The statement of the Assistant
Secretary for Near Eastern and South Asian affairs,
Joseph Sisco, set forth "the very, very significant" political and economic interests the U.S. re-
putedly had at stake in the region.  They were as
follows:

    (1)Support for indigenous regional col-
    lective security efforts to provide sta-
    bility and to foster orderly development
    without outside interference.
    (2)The peaceful resolution of territorial
    and other disputes among the regional
    states and the opening up of better channels
    of communication among them.
    (3)Continued access to Gulf oil supplies
    at reasonable prices and in sufficient quan-
    tities to meet our growing needs and those
    of our European and Asian friends and al-
    lies.
    (4)Enhancing of our commercial and finan-
    cial interests.(14)

    With some overlap James Noyes as the Defense

Department spokesman, defined U.S. security interests in the Gulf as follows:

(1)Containment of Soviet military power within its present borders;
(2)access to Persian Gulf oil; and
(3)continued free movement of United States ships and aircraft into and out of the area.(15)

Several contextual aspects of these two policy statements require comment. Under the Nixon administration the U.S. embarked on a loosely defined "detente" relationship with the Soviet Union. At the Moscow summit in May 1972 the two superpowers promulgated a "statement of basic principles," which if adhered to, promised to revolutionize their relationship.(16) In the nuclear age there was "no alternative," they said, to mutual acceptance of a policy of "peaceful coexistence." Both acknowledged their "special responsibility" as permanent members of the United Nations Security Council to do "everything in their power" to avoid conflict situations that increased international tensions. Both would seek to settle future differences by peaceful means. Neither power would claim special rights for itself, nor take "unilateral advantage" at the expense of the other.
In the Middle East they accepted U.N. Resolution 242 as the appropriate basis for settlement of the Arab-Israeli dispute, which once attained was expected to lead to a further military relaxation. In the 1970s the Middle East including the Persian Gulf region was to provide a severe test for implementation of the Moscow "basic principles." Were they intrinsically incompatible with "containment of Soviet military power" referred to in Noyes' statement and access to Persian Gulf oil, cited by both Noyes and Sisco? By the end of the

decade many observers were inclined to render an affirmative answer to the first question and harbored serious doubts about the ultimate answer to the second.

Another contextual element was the fundamental shift in the world oil market from a buyer's to a seller's market in the early 1970s. The demand for oil which had radically increased in the last decade in both the industrial and developing countries was emphatically registered in the United States. At the same time the once powerful international oil companies with their important American components were undergoing a process of rapid nationalization by Middle Eastern oil countries. Under the impact of these two trends the Organization of Petroleum Exporting Countries(OPEC), which had previously played a relatively minor role in world oil transactions, became a powerful cartel to which oil consuming countries were increasingly beholden. The wider political implications of OPEC's growing influence became evident during the October 1973 Arab-Israeli war, when Arab members of OPEC imposed a damaging oil embargo on the U.S. in retaliation for American support of the Israeli cause. It became an open question whether the abstemious use of American military power contemplated under the Nixon Doctrine would suffice to cope with sudden interruptions of Middle East oil imports in the future, whether instigated by regional oil producers or by Soviet initiatives in the Gulf.


*The U.S. Two-Pillar Policy*

Washington's intention to rely on "indigenous collective security efforts" to provide regional security was shortly more sharply defined. In the early 1970s two of the Gulf states--Iran and Saudi Arabia, became the primary focus of U.S. policy in the Gulf. The rationale for what became known as the U.S. "two-pillar" policy was threefold: (1)the U.S. had enjoyed close relations with both Iran and Saudi Arabia for more than two decades, hence they were expected to serve as reliable regional surrogates; (2)both Iran and Saudi Arabia as conservative monarchial states shared American anxieties regarding future Soviet expansion in the region; and (3)Iran's burgeoning military power combined with Saudi Arabia's financial assets, enhanced by rising oil prices, would constitute a formidable, if indirect instrument of American policy in the Gulf.

Considerable evidence exists that certain implications of the two-pillar policy were not fully canvassed by policymakers in the Nixon administration. In practice Iranian military strength could not be readily equated with Saudi financial power; critical reference was sometimes slightingly made to Washington's "one-and-a-half pillar" policy. The leading assumption that non-Arab Iran could form a functioning partnership with the Arab Saudi state was dubious. Certain Iranian policies caused apprehension among Gulf Arabs that the Shah was bent on regional hegemony. These included Iran's seizure of strategically located Abu Musa and Tunbs Islands at the entrance of the Gulf in 1971; its long-standing territorial claims against Bahrain, deferred under U.N. prodding in 1970; the Shah's frequently voiced warning that neither superpower was welcome as Britain's successor in the Gulf coupled with initial Iranian opposition to a continued U.S. naval presence in Bahrain; and the systematic buildup of Iranian naval forces to reinforce Iran's leadership claims in the Gulf. Finally the inherent weakness of a surrogate policy was not initially appreciated--that the chosen local agent of American policy may either shift his own originally pro-Western stance or himself suffer a fall from power. Only at the end of the decade did the U.S. acknowledge the heavy costs of pursuing this policy option.

The sections which follow deal with certain aspects of the two-pillar policy as it developed in the Nixon-Ford administrations between 1971-76. They include the following topics: (1)various aspects of U.S. relations with the two regional surrogates; (2)relations between the two surrogates; (3)the extension of U.S. arms assistance to other Gulf states; (4)critical reactions in the U.S. Congress to an executive-dominated Gulf policy; and (5)a summation statement on the two-pillar policy.


## (1)  *U.S. Relations with Iran*

*The Pre-1971 Period*

Before Iran attained the status of regional surrogate in the 1970s the U.S. had maintained a complex set of relationships with Iran for more than two decades. In the aftermath of World War II the U.S. led the opposition in the United Nations to continued presence of Soviet troops in northern Iran and creation of a Soviet puppet regime in Azerbaijan province. In the early 1950s the U.S. became deeply involved in Iran's internal politics, climaxed by the decisive role of the Central Intelligence Agency(CIA) in overthrowing nationalist Premier Mohammed Mossadegh in 1953, enabling the Shah to remain in power. Later the CIA helped organize the notorious Iranian secret police known as SAVAK, which was a major prop of the Shah's regime. In 1955 Iran joined the U.S. sponsored Baghdad Pact, in which it became a pivotal member after Iraq's abrupt withdrawal in 1958. In 1959 this connection with Washington was reinforced by a bilateral defense agreement, which declared firm U.S. support for Iranian independence and integrity.(17)

Certain strains marked this developing relationship. U.S. policymakers were intermittently critical of the Shah's seemingly insatiable demands for arms shipments under an expanding program of U.S. grant aid. Would the Shah's escalating requirements for arms imports not have a disjunctive effect on the Iranian economy? Was he capable of stable long-term leadership in the face of mounting internal opposition? The Shah made skillful use of leverage on the U.S. which periodic Soviet efforts to move him into their orbit afforded him. In the Kennedy administration continued U.S. aid was made contingent on reduction in the size of Iran's armed forces and adoption of social and economic reforms designed to increase the Shah's popular support. Ironically, the Shah's "White Revolution" in 1962-63 including a highly controversial land reform program engendered a storm of domestic protest which the Shah suppressed by force. These events were the seedbed of the revolutionary movement that led to the Shah's downfall in 1979.

In the Johnson administration a military sales agreement with Iran in 1964 set up a four-year plan providing for up to $50 million a year in arms transfers, which after two years was increased to $100 million a year. Each year U.S. officials were to undertake a critical assessment of the impact of these military purchases on Iran's economic and social programs.(18) A substantial increase in Iran's gross national product and industrial production in the late 1960s led to the termination of U.S. grant aid in 1969. This foreshadowed a new era in U.S.-Iranian relations. Future Iranian arms purchases were placed on a cash basis which implied few restrictions on the range and quantity of Iran's arms imports. As Iran's oil revenues rapidly expanded in the early 1970s, the stage was set for an impressive buildup in Iran's armed forces and a massive program of arms purchases.

## Iran as Regional Surrogate

The close U.S.-Iranian relationship formed in the Nixon administration rested on a temporary convergence of mutual national interest. In applying the Nixon Doctrine to the Persian Gulf the U.S. required a militarily strong and politically compatible regional state to fill the power vacuum left by the British withdrawal in 1971, lest it be filled by an expansionist Soviet Union or Soviet proxy. Iran was seen as a particularly appropriate candidate. Oil-rich Iran could fill the power vacuum with a minimal expenditure of U.S. resources and a relatively small number of American technical personnel.(19)

U.S. objectives meshed with those of the Shah: his insistence that non-regional states be disqualified to fill the power vacuum in the Gulf and his ambitions to serve as Gulf policeman and preserve the conservative status quo against radical claimants like Iraq and the PFLOAG liberation movement. As the U.S. agreed to supply Iran with increasing amounts of technologically advanced weapons, Iran could even hope to free itself from past dependency on the U.S. in the not distant future. In the interval, even if prolonged close U.S.-Iranian relations would be mutually supportive.

Over the next five years the most striking features of the Washington-Teheran axis were the unprecedented magnitude and high technological level of weapons which the U.S. supplied Iran, the rapid growth of an "American presence" in Iran inexorably linked to the Shah's domestic programs, U.S. support for several of Iran's important external activities and certain joint U.S.-Iranian projects inside Iran.

The special character of the Nixon administration's policy was established in May 1972, when the President and his adviser Henry Kissinger, returning from the Moscow summit with Leonid Brezhnev, visited the Shah in Teheran. Nixon reassured the Shah that the U.S. and the Soviets were not engaged in dividing the world into American and Russian spheres of influence in which Iran's vital interests would be sacrificed. Indeed Washington was willing to grant the Shah a virtual *carte blanche* in arms purchases, save for nuclear weapons, provide technicians to train Iran's armed forces in the use and maintenance of advanced weapons, and underwrite Iran's support for the Kurdish nationalist insurgency against Iraq. All three promises were subsequently implemented.

Previously officials in the U.S. Defense Department had cautioned against an open-ended commitment by the U.S. Iran's utility as a regional surrogate might diminish, it was argued, by the time certain advanced equipment like F-14 and F-15 planes were actually delivered to Iran. Information on U.S. advanced weaponry under Iran's control might leak to the Soviet Union. In July 1972 Kissinger issued a policy guideline for the National Security Council, stating that "decisions on the acquisition of military equipment should be left primarily to the Government of Iran."(20) Defense and State department reviews of subsequent arms transfers to Iran became perfunctory.


*Arming Iran*

From 1950 to 1971 U.S. arms sales to Iran were limited to $1.2 billion. Over a five-year period between 1971-76 the cumulative total was nearly $12 billion. The increase following the quadrupling of world oil prices after the October 1973 Arab-Israeli war was especially dramatic. In 1972 U.S. arms sales to Iran were $519 million, in 1973 $2.2 billion, and in 1974 $4.3 billion.(21) In the 1970s the U.S. sales program to Iran was the largest in the world.

The Iranian air force and navy were major recipients of U.S. military equipment.(22) The most advanced U.S. fighters in the F-14 and F-16 series were purchased as well as an elaborate air defense system using surface-to-air missiles and new long-range transport aircraft. Four Spruance-class destroyers in a more advanced model than the U.S. Navy itself was using and three diesel submarines were purchased for the navy. In addition U.S.-supplied tanks were an important component of the army's growing strength. The Shah himself maintained close supervision over the purchase of all U.S. equipment, summing up his role as follows: "The arms I choose. All the systems I choose." (23)

Few Iranians were qualified to handle and service such advanced weaponry. A rapidly expanding influx of American technical personnel, both military and civilian, proved necessary. From 1972 until the middle of 1976, the resident American community in Iran increased from 15,000 to 31,000 persons.(24) Half of the American community was from the U.S. private sector. A number of American private companies engaged in the actual training of Iranian military personnel or maintenance of military equipment. These included the Bell Helicopter Company, who contracted to train 1,500 helicopter pilots and 5,000 mechanics, and McDonnell-Douglas that did airplane maintenance for the Iranian Air Force.(25) Two characteristics of this American enclave, concentrated chiefly in

the capital of Teheran, had political overtones.
One was the Americans' marked tendency to live in
isolated communities, rarely speaking the Farsi
language of most Iranians, inadequately briefed in
the complexities of Muslim culture in Iran. Sec-
ondly to many Iranians the Americans became closely
identified with negative features of the Pahlavi
regime, its increasingly repressive and dictatorial
character, its commitment to excessively rapid economic development, the grave imbalance of governmental expenditures in favor of the military. The
incipient Iranian revolution was acquiring a highly
visible foreign target.


*Helping the Kurdish Rebels*

   A seemingly extraneous aspect of the U.S. decision in 1972 to supply the Shah with virtually
unlimited arms was a pledge to support Iranian assistance to the Kurdish revolt against Iraq. For
decades the Kurds, a non-Arab people living in the
mountainous border regions of Iraq, Turkey, and
Iran, had sought to establish an autonomous government. Iran's arming of the Kurdish rebels in Iraq
was partly undertaken as retaliation for Iraq's
encouragement of the Arab minority in Iran's critical oil-producing province of Khuzistan. Iran's
special problem was to support the Iraqi Kurds
without inadvertently encouraging a revolt by its
own Kurdish population, whose size approximated
the two million Kurds in Iraq.
   The U.S. effort on behalf of the Kurdish revolt in Iraq was undertaken in considerable se-
crecy.(26) Both the State department and the CIA
had serious reservations regarding U.S. involvement. Kissinger did not submit the matter for
discussion by the National Security Council or the
Forty Committee on covert operations. Former

Treasury Secretary John Connally was entrusted
with a special mission to Teheran to inform the
Shah the U.S. was starting arms deliveries to the
Kurds. In due course the CIA supplied the Kurdish rebels with large stores of Soviet and Chi-
nese weapons captured mostly in Vietnam. Kissinger
later claimed a short-term payoff for the U.S. when
embattled Iraq could not make a major contribution
in the October 1973 Middle East war.(27)

Early in 1975 the Shah abruptly terminated
his support for the Kurdish rebels. At an OPEC
conference in Algiers in March under the good of-
fices of Algerian President Houari Boumedienne
the Iranian Shah held talks with Iraq's Saddam
Hussein. The two leaders not only promised to
stop supporting each other's enemies, but also
agreed to settle their long-standing border dispute over the Shatt al-Arab estuary at the head of
the Gulf. The Shah immediately sealed his border
with Iraq, insuring the collapse of the Kurdish
revolt. Surprised by the Shah's sudden shift in
policy, Washington had little choice except to
suspend its own covert operations on behalf of the
Kurdish nationalists.

*The Shah as Gulf Policeman*

With the departure of the British from the
Gulf in 1971 the Shah was acutely conscious of the
danger of a sudden takeover by hostile forces of
the Strait of Hormuz at the entrance to the Gulf.
If such an action succeeded, the movement of Iran's
vitally important oil exports would be halted. To
forestall such an eventuality the Shah was willing
to risk the displeasure of his Gulf Arab neighbors
by forcibly seizing the strategically located Abu
Musa and Tunb islands in 1971. Significantly
Washington acquiesced in this unilateral action by
the Shah.

The single most important instance of Iran's policing role was the Shah's collaboration with Sultan Qabus of Oman in crushing the Dhofar rebellion between 1973-76, their joint effort being endorsed by the U.S. The two rulers shared a strong antipathy to Marxist-oriented revolutionary movements like the Omani PFLOAG. Initially the PFLOAG anticipated that its projected overthrow of the Sultan's government would trigger off successful revolutions in neighboring Gulf sheikdoms, an abhorrent prospect to the Shah.(28) Over three thousand Iranian troops were subsequently dispatched to Oman. The Shah arranged for periodic rotation of the Iranian contingent in Oman, affording a segment of the Iranian army valuable battlefield experience. Early in 1975 Iran and Oman extended their military cooperation to conducting joint naval operations in the Strait of Hormuz.

The Dhofar rebellion precipitated a revealing alignment of conservative and radical forces in the Gulf. In addition to Iranian troops Sultan Qabus was aided by the expertise of British and Pakistani officers attached to the Omani armed forces. Jordan sent an Army battalion and a shipment of Hawker fighter aircraft. The U.S. sent TOW anti-tank missiles with two instructors. In the opposing camp the Dhofar rebels were logistically based in Marxist South Yemen, which bordered on Oman. The Soviet Union also materially supported the rebel cause as did its client, Baathist Iraq. In early 1975 Libya's Colonel Qaddafi demanded an Iranian troop withdrawal from Oman and threatened Libyan intervention if "foreign forces" remained in Oman. But with substantial outside assistance Sultan Qabus was enabled to defeat the Dhofar rebellion. A cease-fire came into effect in 1976, and Iranian forces were withdrawn by early 1977. In retrospect quelling the Marxist revolutionary threat in Oman constituted an exemplary application of the Nixon

Doctrine to the Gulf region. Yet even now a future
outbreak of the Omani revolt remains a definite
possibility.

Repeated Iranian attempts to form a regional
defense pact comprised of Iran and the Gulf Arab
States proved unavailing. Two rounds of talks in
which all the Gulf states were participants were
held before the collapse of the Shah's regime.
Progress at the first meeting held in Kuwait in
July 1974 was hampered by an unresolved border dispute between Kuwait and Iraq. The second meeting
held in Oman in November 1976 was inconclusive as
the participants failed to agree on the subject of
intelligence data sharing. But the fundamental obstacle to effective regional security arrangements
was continued Arab apprehension of Iranian domination of Gulf affairs.


*U.S.-Iranian Joint Endeavors*

Two other important forms of U.S.-Iranian
cooperation under the Nixon-Ford administrations
require mention. A wide range of joint intelligence activities was seen by both states as mutually beneficial. These included the establishment
of border listening posts to intercept Soviet communications and facilitate American monitoring of
Soviet missile tests, reconnaissance missions into
Soviet territory, setting up escape routes for Soviet defectors headed for Western countries, and
sharing intelligence estimates of countries important to both the U.S. and Iran.(29) An example
of involvement by the U.S. private sector was the
1975 agreement made by the Iranian government with
Rockwell International for the latter to build an
intelligence facility that could intercept military and civilian communications in the Persian
Gulf area. As internal opposition to the Shah

mounted, SAVAK agents were allowed to enter the
U.S. for purposes of surveillance over Iranian
students and to counteract anti-Shah demonstrations
in the U.S.

In 1974 a joint U.S.-Iranian economic commission was set up and an American trade center opened
in Teheran to facilitate expansion in trade relations. Early in 1975 the two countries signed a
trade agreement, which envisioned $15 billion in
commerce over a five-year period, one-third of it
in petroleum. In exchange the U.S. would provide
eight nuclear power stations and their fuel, pre-
fabricated housing, hospitals, ports, electrical
equipment, fertilizers, pesticides, farm machinery,
superhighways, and a vocational training center.(30)
This agreement reflected an uncritical U.S. assessment of the Shah's highly controversial program of
rapid economic development. A supplementary trade
protocol in 1976 raised the five-year trading goal
to $52 billion.

Despite these striking instances of mutuality
of interest between the U.S. and Iran their relationship was not free of serious frictions. At the
important OPEC conference held in Teheran in 1971
the Shah took the lead in proposing a significant
increase in oil prices from 30 to 50 cents a barrel.
In spite of Iran's long-standing position as the
chief oil supplier to Israel the Shah made it clear
he would support the Arab cause if Washington
failed to heed his requests for expanded arms shipments. When the Arab oil-producing countries imposed an oil embargo on the U.S. during the October
1973 war, the Shah abstained from the embargo. But
he enthusiastically supported OPEC's quadrupling
in oil prices, and subsequently became known as a
leading "price hawk" in OPEC deliberations.

## (2)  *U.S. Relations with Saudi Arabia*

*The Pre-1971 Period*

Oil, strategic considerations and the Palestine issue have served as constituent elements of the "special relationship" between the U.S. and Saudi Arabia since its inception during World War II.  In 1943 Saudi Arabia was declared eligible for U.S. lend-lease assistance as a means of securing the existing American stake in Saudi oil represented by the exclusively U.S.-owned ARAMCO company.(31)  In the same year a special U.S. mission was sent to Saudi Arabia to determine its military requirements.

At the war-time meeting of Ibn Saud and Franklin Roosevelt in 1945 the future status of Palestine, then under British mandate, proved a contentious issue.  The Saudi ruler was adamantly opposed to creation of an independent Jewish state in Palestine at the end of the war.  Roosevelt assured Ibn Saud that the U.S. would not take any steps on the Palestine question that were hostile to the Arab people and promised consultations with the Arabs before making a final decision.(32) Roosevelt's successor Truman proved more amenable to Zionist pressure when Israel became independent in 1948.

At the end of the war some U.S. officials manifested increased concern over sharply declining oil reserves which would confront the U.S. in the next 25 years.  Defense Secretary James V. Forrestal was a leading articulator of the view that assured petroleum supplies were an indispensable condition for U.S. survival in future wars.  Forrestal stressed the importance of Saudi oil reserves, stating that "I don't care which American company or companies develop the Arabian reserves, but I think most emphatically that it should be *Ameri-*

can."(33)   In 1950 the Saudi government reached
agreement with ARAMCO which provided for a 50-50
splitting of pre-tax profits.  Saudi oil revenues
from ARAMCO were at once substantially increased--
from $56 million in 1950 to $110 million in 1951.
     Beginning in 1946 the Saudis permitted the
U.S. Air Force "unrestricted air traffic rights"
at Dhahran airfield on a temporary basis.  The
Dhahran base later became an important link in the
U.S. global network of strategic bases directed
against the Soviet bloc.  Under a mutual defense
agreement in 1951 the leasing of the Dhahran base
was linked to U.S. shipments of military equipment
and setting up a military training mission in
Saudi Arabia, financed by U.S. grant aid. Persist-
ing Saudi-U.S. differences over Israel's existence
as an independent state clouded their relationship.
After some hesitation Saudi Arabia renewed the U.S.
lease of Dhahran airfield for a five-year period
in 1956.  But in 1962 the U.S. lost the use of this
important military installation.
     Fresh strains in the U.S.-Saudi relationship
appeared in the early 1960s when Saudi Arabia and
Nasserite Egypt intervened on opposing sides in the
civil war in North Yemen.  The Saudis favored the
Yemeni Royalists, while Egypt gave military support
to the Republican rebels.  In 1962 the decision of
the Kennedy administration to recognize the Yemeni
Republicans was ill-received in Riyadh.  But Kennedy's willingness to send fighter aircraft to
Saudi Arabia after Egyptian attacks on Saudi territory somewhat eased these strained relations.  Further improvement occurred under the Johnson administration when Crown Prince Faisal succeeded the
hapless King Saud in 1964.  Faisal embarked on a
modest program of modernization and development
which Washington welcomed.  In 1965 the U.S. and
Britain entered into an important joint agreement
to assist in the modernization of the Saudi armed

forces. The principal U.S. contribution was to
supply the Saudis with basic Hawk missile batter-
ies for air defense purposes.

The imposition of a brief oil embargo during
the 1967 Arab-Israeli war in which Saudi Arabia
participated provided an ominous portent for the
future. For the first time Arab oil-producing
countries shut down all their oil production. In
this heated atmosphere bands of saboteurs assembled with explosives, prepared to destroy Western
oil installations.(34)  Saudi Arabia government
troops moved in to prevent acts of sabotage. The
1967 oil embargo was too short to have serious effects on U.S.-Saudi relations.

*Expanding the "Special Relationship"*

Even though Saudi Arabia was destined to play
a definitely subordinate role to Iran under the
U.S. two-pillar policy, its long-standing "special
relationship" with the U.S. was significantly amplified after 1971. Paralleling U.S. policy in
Iran the expanded U.S. relationship with Saudi Arabia was marked by a massive increase in U.S. arms
shipments financed by Saudi Arabia's very large oil
revenues, an enlarged "American presence," and an
intricate financial relationship. U.S. policy was
based on acceptance of Saudi Arabia's security requirements derived from having a relatively small
population in a vast country and its long exposed
land borders and 2,000 miles of coastline along the
Persian Gulf and Red Sea. Its location between the
radical Baathist regime in Iraq to the north and
the Marxist PDRY in the southwest, both client
states of the Soviet Union, was viewed as politically precarious. Saudi Arabia also shared the
same strongly anti-Communist view held by successive U.S. administrations and was valued as a leading "moderate" on the Arab side in the Palestine

question and as capable of exercising influence in the strategically located Arab sheikdoms on the Gulf.

In the early 1970s the U.S. became deeply involved in all aspects of Saudi Arabia's comprehensive program of military modernization. As in the case of Iran, there was a spectacular increase in U.S. arms sales and contracts for training personnel between 1971 and 1976, totalling over $7 billion. Following the big increase in the world price of oil in 1973-74 arm sales to Saudi Arabia jumped from $709 million in 1973 to over $2.5 billion in 1974.(35) A distinctive feature of the U.S. program for Saudi Arabia was the much higher percentage of nearly 80 percent in so-called "software" training and construction over the roughly 20 percent for "hardware," i.e. arms and equipment. This was reflected in the central role of the U.S. Corps of Engineers who carried out a remarkably far-ranging construction program. This included the building of military cantonments at strategically located points, family housing for dependents of military personnel, airports, deep-water ports as well as schools and hospitals. An estimated 90 percent of the Corps' construction activity was military related.

The unfolding pattern of U.S. involvement in the Saudis' military modernization was cyclical in nature. The initial step was a series of Defense Department surveys which came to be regarded as military blueprints by Saudi planners. To implement the surveys large-scale imports of military equipment were required. Due to the paucity of Saudi technicians the imported military equipment had to be installed and subsequently maintained by foreign personnel. Saudi soldiers in all three branches of the armed forces had to be trained by outside technicians. It proved impractical to set terminal dates for completion of these several loosely integrated programs, so an almost indefinite extension of the "special relationship" with the U.S. appeared likely.

U.S. military planners had to take into account the special characteristics and division of labor between the Saudi Army and National Guard. The Army of approximately 30,000 troops was responsible for national defense. The National Guard of some 20,000 soldiers representing tribal units close to the Royal family was charged with internal security and served as a backstop army in defending the national borders.(36) The National Guard owed its privileged position partly to the high status of its commander Prince Abdullah, who had direct access to the Saudi monarch. Under an agreement made in 1973 the U.S. agreed to organize, equip, and train four mechanized infantry battalions for the National Guard.(37) The end result was to transform the Guard from a paramilitary unit to a mobile striking force, seen as critical for the continued tenure of the Royal family. In the case of the Army the U.S. assisted in converting two infantry brigades to mechanized units.

In 1971 the U.S. agreed to equip the Saudi Air Force with F-5 planes and train Saudi personnel to maintain them, which was expected to take close to a generation. In 1972 the U.S. agreed to participate in a 10-year program to modernize the relatively small Saudi Navy. Twenty-five ships were to be added to the original fleet of four ships. This included 13 patrol gunboats which were expected to comprise the "core" element of the Navy. Over a 5 year period 2,000 Saudi sailors were to be sent mostly to the U.S. for training purposes. In the 1970s an overall total of 5,000 Saudi personnel received military training in the U.S.

Since the U.S. Defense department was willing to assign only a limited number of American military technicians to Saudi Arabia, private American contractors played an extremely important role in the Saudi training program.(38) The Vinnel Corporation contracted to train four battalions of the National Guard, and Bendix provided training in maintenance and supply operations for the Guard's artillery unit. Northrup Corporation contracted to train personnel in the Air Force to fly and maintain F-5 fighters. By 1976 an estimated 30,000 Americans were working in Saudi Arabia with over 20 percent in defense related projects. Even more than in Iran local contacts were extremely limited for most Americans. The strict Wahhabi code was not compatible with a relatively uninhibited American life style. As was true in Iran Islamic fundamentalists are strongly critical of the alien American presence.

Since 1971 the U.S.-Saudi economic connection has become increasingly complicated. With the phenomenal rise in oil prices the U.S. sought to lessen its balance-of-payment difficulties by encouraging the investment of Saudi "petrodollars" in the U.S. economy. At the same time many Americans manifested antipathy to large-scale Arab investment in U.S. businesses and real estate. Saudi investments have tended to be limited to short-term certificates of deposit and Treasury bills.

Along with a Joint Commission on security affairs a second Joint Commission for economic cooperation were set up in 1974. On the economic commission joint working groups were subsequently established in the fields of industrialization, manpower and education, science and technology, and agriculture. Private American consultants advised the Saudis on successive five-year plans. In 1975 U.S. companies were awarded over $25 billion in contracts under the five-year plan then in effect, and U.S. participation in the developing petrochemical industry was encouraged. As in the case of Pahlavi Iran this trend of heavy U.S. economic involvement carries the risk of excessively close American identification with the domestic policies of the Saudi government.

*Frictions in the "Special Relationship"*

In the Arab oil embargo imposed during the 1967 Arab-Israeli war Saudi Arabia was a somewhat reluctant accessory, prodded by President Nasser of Egypt. In the far more effective oil embargo initiated in the October 1973 war Saudi Arabia played the leading role. Several factors explain the difference. Nasser had died in 1970. His successor, Anwar Sadat had severed Egypt's once close connection with the Soviet Union and was pursuing national policies significantly less radical than Nasser's. Saudi Arabia's relations with Egypt, previously troubled, improved very considerably. In King Faisal's view an Arab oil embargo would now be less subject to manipulation by radical Arab forces. The U.S. position in 1973 was also different from that in 1967. In 1967 the U.S. had been only marginally involved in the oil embargo, coming to the succor of other Western countries. In the interval the U.S. had become a major importer of Middle Eastern oil and would certainly be adversely affected by another cutoff in oil imports. By 1973 the U.S. was using 2.5 million barrels of Arab oil a day either for domestic consumption or for its military forces abroad. Finally Saudi Arabia was by 1973 receiving vastly increased oil revenues and better able to withstand a temporary reduction in oil sales.

Immediately prior to the 1973 war King Faisal issued a public warning that continued American support for Israel "makes it extremely difficult for us to continue to supply the United States' petroleum needs and even to maintain friendly relations."(39) In 1973 Saudi Arabia was producing

47

42 percent of the Arab countries' oil production, which placed Riyadh in a favorable position to play a decisive role in the use of oil as a political weapon.

The 1973 oil embargo was imposed as a result of Washington's decision to resupply Israel with arms during the October war. On October 17 the Organization of Arab Petroleum Exporting Countries (OAPEC) meeting in Kuwait decided to cut oil production monthly by 5 percent over the previous month's sales until Israel had withdrawn from the occupied Arab territories and agreed to respect the rights of Palestinian refugees.(40)

The following day Saudi Arabia announced it would cut back its oil production by 10 percent and cut off all shipments to the U.S., if the Nixon administration continued to supply Israel with arms and failed to modify its pro-Israel policy. The administration under pressure of the pro-Israeli lobby in Washington followed the opposite course. On October 19 President Nixon asked Congress for a $2.2 billion appropriation for emergency military aid to Israel. Earlier the Soviet Union had launched an emergency military airlift to the Arab side. Saudi Arabia then announced a total oil embargo against the U.S. The Saudi action was supported by Kuwait, Bahrain, Dubai, Abu Dhabi and Qatar, and was in effect for a five-month period.

The OAPEC members applied the embargo differentially according to certain categories. Nations considered to be "friends of Israel" were subject to a total boycott--the U.S. and the Netherlands. Later Portugal, Rhodesia, and South Africa were added to the boycott list. Oil shipments to Canada were halted as the Arabs feared they would be reshipped to the U.S. Exempted nations included France, Spain, other Arab and Muslim countries and on a conditional basis, Britain. The third category of "non-exempted" countries was allowed to purchase whatever oil was left after the needs of "exempted" countries were met.

OAPEC's drastic action precipitated a crisis between the U.S. and its allies, most of whom were more vulnerable to Arab cutbacks in oil production than the U.S. Representatives of the European Economic Community(EEC) meeting in Brussels in November called on Israel "to end its territorial occupation" of the West Bank and Gaza imposed in the 1967 war and stated that any Arab-Israeli settlement would have to take into account the "legitimate rights" of the Palestinian refugees.(41) Japan also shifted to a position critical of Israel. These Western European nations and Japan were exempted from the 5 percent Arab oil cutback in December.

The oil embargo also adversely affected the U.S. domestic economy which according to some estimates suffered a deficiency of about two million barrels of oil a day. Over a five-month period the embargo cost a half-million American jobs and a decline in the gross national product of between $10-20 billion.(42) Some Arab oil reportedly leaked through to the U.S. from Libya and Iraq.

The distinctive feature of the 1973 embargo --the cutback in production, facilitated the simultaneous quadrupling of oil prices by OPEC. Just prior to the October war OPEC negotiators were planning to induce the international oil companies to accept a doubling in the $3 a barrel price. In the course of the October war in a series of unilateral actions OPEC increased the oil price from $3 a barrel in October to $11.65 a barrel in December. To some economists this radical price increase was a major factor in the worldwide recession in 1974-75.

Although Secretary of State Kissinger publicly insisted that no linkage existed between an Arab-Israeli settlement and the unimpeded flow of Arab oil to the West, there appears to be an irrefutable connection between Kissinger's "shuttle diplomacy" during and after the October war and OAPEC's decision to lift the oil embargo in March 1974. Kissinger's efforts to mediate a settlement were marked by a series of crisscross flights to Israeli and Arab capitals, resulting in several limited agreements. These included a November 11 cease-fire agreement in the 1973 war between Israel and Egypt, the first round of Arab-Israeli peace talks in Geneva on December 21-22, and two disengagement agreements in 1974--first between Egypt and Israel on January 18 and then between Syria and Israel on May 31.(43)

After the first disengagement agreement President Sadat observed that "now that the Americans have made a gesture, the Arabs should make one, too," an obvious reference to the oil embargo. In Washington the Saudi and Egyptian ambassadors reportedly urged the administration "to do something for Syria." The Arab oil producers at a meeting in Vienna March 17 lifted the oil embargo. The Syrian-Israeli agreement followed in May. The original Arab goal of enforcing Israeli withdrawal from the occupied territories was obviously not attained. But the Vienna communique of the Arab oil ministers reiterated the Arab call for "complete" Israeli withdrawal, clearly implying a continued linkage between a final Arab-Israeli settlement and future recourse to the oil weapon.

The severity of the 1973 oil embargo stimulated an acrimonious discussion in the U.S. as to the possible range of U.S. actions, should the Arab states again impose an oil embargo. Influential voices were raised to urge the use of U.S. military force in the Gulf oil fields if such an eventuality arose.(44) Predictably threats of Western military intervention provoked hostile responses from Saudi Arabia and other Arab oil producers.

Several of the tactics employed by the Nixon-Ford administrations after the 1973 war to meet the challenge of an emboldened OPEC were confrontational. In sponsoring the organization of the International Energy Agency(IEA) the U.S. was partly intending to confront the oil-producing countries with the presumed solidarity of oil consumers. After Vice-President Gerald Ford succeeded to the presidency in 1974 both he and Secretary Kissinger made speeches linking oil prices to food export prices, which Arab oil producers interpreted as "intimidation" by the West.

Extremely negative reactions in the Middle East followed Kissinger's widely publicized interview in *Business Week* in January 1975. Asked whether he would consider military action by the U.S. on oil prices, Kissinger replied, "I am not saying that there is no circumstance where we would not use force. But it is one thing to use it in the case of dispute over price, it's another whether there is some actual strangulation of the industrialized world."(45) Later Kissinger qualified his comment by stating the latter contingency would arise only if the U.S. were involved in a war situation.

In December 1976 Saudi Arabia took an important step in directly linking oil prices with the Arab-Israeli conflict. At an OPEC conference in Qatar, Saudi Arabia raised its oil price by 5 percent in contrast with a two-stage increase of 15 percent by 11 other OPEC members. The Saudi minister of petroleum, Sheik Yamani, pointedly indicated that the U.S. was expected to show "appreciation" for the lower Saudi increase by inducing Israel to make appropriate concessions on the occupied territories.(46)

## (3)  *Iranian-Saudi Relations*

A major assumption of the U.S. two-pillar policy was that the Shah of Iran and the Saudis would
form a working partnership as regional surrogates
of Washington. But it became an open question
whether cooperative or competitive elements would
prevail in their relationship. The relatively
brief period of 1971-77 before Iran entered a
stage of revolutionary turmoil did not provide a
conclusive answer, but in retrospect collaboration between the two surrogates appears to have
been limited.(47)

Certain underlying differences created a formidable obstacle to a fully effective partnership.
If Saudi Arabia is assumed to have a population of
between five and six million (estimates vary),
Iran's population is roughly six times larger.
While both are physically large states their distinctive locations carry different political implications. Saudi Arabia is on the Arabian peninsula and is preoccupied with other states on the
peninsula and the Horn of Africa across the Strait
of Bab al-Mandeb. Although separated from Saudi
Arabia by only a narrow stretch of water in the
Gulf, Iran has to consider a larger geopolitical
context including its long border with the Soviet
Union and its proximity to Iraq, Turkey, Afghanistan, and Pakistan. The economies of both states
are heavily dependent on oil production, but Saudi
Arabia has "proved and probable" reserves of crude
oil several times greater than Iran. Between 1972
and 1977 Saudi oil production increased at an annual rate of 9.8 percent as compared to 2.4 percent
for Iran, giving Saudi Arabia additional leverage
in OPEC deliberations. Profound cultural differences divide the two states especially in their
religious affiliations--Shia predominance in Iran,

Sunni Muslim in Saudi Arabia. Tensions between the Persian Empire and the Arab world are long-standing, aggravated in the 1970s by Iran's hegemonic aspirations in the Gulf. At the personal level the Shah and Crown Prince Fahd were reportedly hard-pressed to conceal their mutual dislike.

These substantial differences were only partially mitigated by certain similarities between the two states. Both had embarked on ambitious programs of economic development based on rapidly increasing oil revenues. The rulers of both states were strongly anti-Communist in outlook, feared Soviet penetration of the Gulf region, and wanted to curb further expansion by Soviet client states like Iraq and South Yemen. Both the Shah and the Saudi royal family were confronted with serious opposition from Islamic fundamentalists who wanted to arrest Western modernization tendencies in their respective countries.

During the 1971-77 period it proved difficult for Iran and Saudi Arabia to coordinate their positions on oil pricing in OPEC, the Arab-Israeli conflict, and regional collective security. In OPEC the two states had serious differences on both the rate of OPEC's periodic increases in oil prices as well as the appropriate level of oil production for a given period. Iranian representatives in OPEC consistently lobbied for a rapid escalation in oil prices, which in part reflected their government's chronic need for increased oil revenues to finance its ambitious development programs and arms purchases. Saudi Arabia, more sensitive to the deleterious effect of high oil prices on the world economy, favored relatively moderate, though still substantial price increases. Iran also pushed for high production levels to maximize government revenues, while Saudi Arabia favored a flexible approach to avoid extreme fluctuations in price.

The OPEC meeting held in Qatar December 1976, cited above, illustrated Saudi-Iranian differences on oil pricing. Most OPEC members including Iran favored an immediate 10 percent price increase to be followed in mid-1977 by another 5 percent increase. Supported only by the UAE, Saudi Arabia held out for a single 5 percent increase. But six months later a compromise was reached to preserve OPEC unity. Saudi Arabia agreed to accept an additional 5 percent increase, and the other OPEC members including Iran accepted a price freeze for the rest of 1977.(48)

On the critical issue of the Arab-Israeli conflict Saudi-Iranian perspectives were substantially different. The Saudis had from the outset opposed the creation of the state of Israel. As keeper of the Muslim holy places Saudi Arabia was particularly concerned with the status of Jerusalem, and after the 1967 war vigorously advocated its return to Arab control. Saudi prestige in the Arab world depended in part on its unwavering support for self-determination of the Palestinian Arabs. Non-Arab Iran was inevitably much less concerned with this issue. Iran had become Israel's main oil supplier, and as early as 1960 accorded Israel *de facto* recognition. In the 1973 Arab-Israeli war Iran, generally opposed to the use of the oil weapon for political purposes, disassociated itself from the Arab oil embargo. Yet Iran supported United Nations Resolution 242 which called for Israel's withdrawal from the occupied territories, and did not grant Israel *de jure* recognition.

The record of Saudi-Iranian collaboration on behalf of regional security was mixed. Both states supported Oman's campaign to quell the Dhofar rebellion--Iran by military intervention, the Saudis with financial support. The security services of the two states exchanged intelligence information. But Saudi Arabia was not sympathetic to the Shah's insistence

that the U.S. was as undesirable a candidate as the
Soviet Union to fill the British vacuum in the Gulf.
Saudi Arabia was less than enthusiastic about Iran's
seizure of three Gulf islands in 1971. Several attempts led by the Shah to form a regional security
organization proved abortive. Like other Gulf states
Saudi Arabia feared that Iran's clear military superiority would insure Iranian domination of such a
regional grouping.

Regional specialists disagree on the impact
of the greatly accelerated U.S. arms sales to both
Iran and Saudi Arabia under the two-pillar policy.
Some experts argued that billion-dollar arms sales
by the U.S. were leading to a serious arms race between the two states which threatened to result in
armed conflict between them. Others pointed to
crucial differentials in U.S. arms sales to the two
countries. In the case of Iran the primary emphasis was on the sale of sophisticated weapons,
whereas Saudi Arabia received mostly "software"--
military construction and training programs. The
inference was that the effect of U.S. sales to the
two countries was non-competitive.


(4) *Extensions in the Two-Pillar Policy*


As the post-1971 U.S. policy on the Gulf unfolded the inexactitude of the "two-pillar" meta-
phor became apparent. Once heavily committed to
Iran and Saudi Arabia U.S. policymakers could
scarcely overlook the larger Gulf context of their
decisions. Would not inexorable logic require the
U.S. to assist at least some of the militarily
weak neighbors of Iran and Saudi Arabia? If so,
additional levels of complexity would necessarily
invest the two-pillar policy. Each of the contacts

the U.S. subsequently established with other Gulf
states had its separate rationale which was then
somewhat loosely fitted into the larger policy.
The gradual process of extending the two-pillar
policy is selectively examined here.

U.S. relations with the island state of Bahrain had a special character. Prior to the independence which Bahrain gained in 1971 Britain controlled its foreign relations. Britain agreed to
share certain port facilities with a small unit of
a half-dozen U.S. Navy ships, designated as Middle
East Force(MIDEASTFOR). This U.S. Navy unit maintained liaison with U.S. diplomatic officials in
the Gulf region, occasionally participated in naval
exercises conducted by the U.S.-sponsored Central
Treaty Organization(CENTO) and was known to have an
intelligence capability. When the British withdrew
from the Gulf in 1971, the U.S. decided to retain
its naval presence in Bahrain as a tangible symbol
of U.S. interest. Thus the U.S. would be enabled
to "show the flag" in a strategically important
area. MIDEASTFOR was simultaneously acquiring
fresh importance as a link to an expanding U.S.
naval force in the Indian Ocean. In December 1971
an agreement was reached with Bahrain which permitted MIDEASTFOR to continue its operations. The
U.S. stressed that its installation there was merely
a logistic "facility" and not a full-fledged "base."
Nor did the U.S. intend to increase its future size
significantly.

Due to the rising tide of Arab nationalism in
the Gulf the position of MIDEASTFOR after 1971
proved precarious.(49) In the 1973 Arab-Israeli
war Bahrain participated in OAPEC's oil embargo
against the U.S. and canceled the 1971 agreement
on MIDEASTFOR. Bahrain rescinded this action late
in 1974 but increased the annual rent charged the
U.S. from $600,000 to $4 million. Partly as a negative response to widespread discussion that the U.S.

might seize the Gulf oil fields in a future emergency the Bahrain government told U.S. officials in 1975 that it intended to phase out the U.S. naval facility by 1977.  In June 1977 Bahrain terminated MIDEASTFOR's lease, but on an informal basis approved its occasional use of Bahraini port facilities.  The future utility of MIDEASTFOR would appear to be minimal.

U.S. interest in the Gulf sheikdom of Kuwait derived from its importance as a major oil exporter, its position in the "moderate" grouping of Arab states and its proximity to anti-Western Iraq at the head of the Gulf.  The extensive military relationship which the U.S. established with Kuwait in the early 1970s was in large measure a function of recurrent acute tensions between Kuwait and Iraq over their unresolved border dispute.

The U.S. took certain steps to bolster Kuwait's defenses.(50)  At the request of the Kuwait government a U.S. Defense department team was sent to Kuwait in 1972 to survey Kuwait's security requirements.  Its principal recommendation was that Kuwait should build up a small operational force that it could eventually maintain without outside help.  After a serious border skirmish with Iraq in March 1973 a second U.S. survey team was sent to Kuwait.  The U.S. recommendation that Kuwait focus its military effort on an effective air defense missile system was accepted by the government.  Between 1973-76 U.S. arms sales to Kuwait totaled $600 million, the most important items being a Hawk Missile system and A-4 aircraft.  About 1,500 Kuwait soldiers received training in the U.S.  But Kuwait jealously guards its independent stance and at times has made overtures to the Soviet Union as an alternative supplier.  Certain frictions have marred the U.S.-Kuwait relationship.  As a prime source of funds for the Palestine Liberation Organization(PLO) Kuwait is a militant sup-

porter of Palestinian self-determination. In OPEC
Kuwait favors rapid escalation in oil prices.

The U.S. relationship with the Sultanate of
Oman rested on the control of the Strait of Hormuz
"choke" point which Oman shares with Iran, the pro-
nounced pro-American sentiments held by its ruler
Sultan Qabus, and Oman's frontline position in opposition to an intermittently active Marxist-type
national liberation movement, the PFLO. In view
of the priority the U.S. accorded its two regional
surrogates--Iran and Saudi Arabia--Washington attempted to maintain a low profile as it entered into relations with Oman. This connection was, however, accelerated by U.S. interest in an early defeat of the leftist Dhofar rebellion in Oman. At
the time of Sultan Qabus' visit to Washington in
January 1975, the U.S. made a sudden decision to
sell TOW missile launchers to Oman, which were airlifted there ten days after the Sultan's visit. In
July 1976 it was announced that U.S. Navy P-3
planes, flying from the U.S. facilities at Diego
Garcia in the Indian Ocean, would be allowed to
make landings for refueling purposes on Masirah
island which was under Oman's jurisdiction.(51)
Consistent with the Nixon Doctrine the U.S. sought
to avoid an overt military presence in Oman. No
U.S. military advisory group was sent there, and
no military representative was assigned to the U.S.
embassy in Muscat.

U.S. interest in the Yemen Arab Republic
(North Yemen) flows from the YAR's strategic location along the Strait of Bab al-Mandeb across from
the Horn of Africa, its close connection with Saudi
Arabia, its vulnerability to pressure from the adjacent Marxist PDRY(South Yemen), and its suscepti-
bility to offers of military and technical assistance from the Soviet Union and its client Iraq.
The gradually evolving military relationship between Washington and Sana, the YAR capital, went

through two phases.(52)  In the 1972-75 period the
U.S. and the YAR maintained a direct relationship,
involving a modest program of U.S. arms sales totalling only $3 million.  Beginning in 1976 there
occurred a shift to an indirect relationship with
Saudi Arabia serving as a filter for U.S. military
aid to North Yemen.  This arrangement reflected the
higher priority the U.S. assigned its relation with
the Saudis.  Based on a military survey done by
U.S. defense specialists, Saudi Arabia devised a
ten-year program of military modernization for the
YAR.  The U.S. undertook a five-year program of arms
sales to North Yemen totalling nearly $140 million,
financed by Saudi Arabia and channeled through the
Saudis.  Fourteen Yemeni officers took training in
the U.S. in 1976.  Significantly North Yemen had
the previous year rejected a Soviet offer of a
$500 million arms package, including the shipment
of Mig 21s.
        U.S. policymakers acknowledged certain prob-
lems in administering the complicated trilateral
military relationship with Saudi Arabia and North
Yemen.  The U.S. had few levers of direct control
to insure the success of its Yemen program.  No
provision covered a possible Saudi decision not to
turn over shipments of U.S. equipment to the Yem-
enis.  If a not altogether unlikely diplomatic
split developed between Saudi Arabia and the YAR,
completion of the U.S. program would be jeopardized.


(5)  *Congressional Criticisms*

        In the post-Vietnam period the U.S. Congress
sought to reassert its traditional prerogatives in
subjecting administration policies to close scrutiny.  This included U.S. policy in the Persian
Gulf in the 1972-76 period.  A regular series of

Congressional hearings especially by the House and Senate foreign affairs committees and a number of special Congressional staff and Library of Congress studies provided the interested public with a substantial amount of information on Gulf policies coupled with measured criticism. By the middle of 1974 Secretary Kissinger, fresh from his diplomatic triumph in the Middle East, held a magisterial position in the government. Even so congressional inquiries on foreign policy persisted. There is, however, little evidence that the administration significantly modified its established policies. In some instances it refused to follow Congressional recommendations. Several important examples of Congressional scrutiny will be examined here.

*The Arms Sales Question*

The whole question of overseas arms sales by the U.S. government received the most Congressional attention. The huge increase in arms sales to Iran and Saudi Arabia coupled with expanding sales to other Gulf countries were a source of special concern. The principal Congressional criticisms of U.S. arms sales in the Gulf can be summarized as follows:(53)

(1)The sheer size of U.S. arms shipments to Iran and Saudi Arabia in view of the Nixon-Ford administration's failure to present convincing evidence that potential threats emanating from the Soviet Union or neighboring Gulf states justified such heavy defense expenditures.
(2)The almost total lack of effective U.S. control over either the quantity

of arms shipments to the two regional surrogates or the qualitatively superior weapons being shipped mostly to Iran. The originally secret decision of the Nixon administration in 1972 to allow the Shah of Iran free rein in selecting non-nuclear weapons provoked strong criticism. It was charged that the executive branch had failed to formulate a specific set of criteria against which the ceaseless flow of foreign arms requests could be carefully weighed, nor were the ultimate consequences of their possible uses properly assessed. Should the U.S., for example, help enlarge the Iranian navy in the Gulf in order to promote the Shah's ambitious foreign policy goals?

(3) Congressional doubts as to the absorptive capacities of recipient countries. Could Iran, for example, afford disproportionately heavy defense expenditures? Would they not create dangerous imbalances between the civilian and military sectors of the national economy?

(4) Questions were raised as to the ultimate impact of the increasing American presence in these countries --the military instructors and technicians, the commercial contractors, and businessmen. If American expatriates became closely identified with unpopular authoritarian governments would not U.S. prestige suffer?

(5) Certain negative aspects of the role of American private contractors in U.S. programs. Cases of bribery

of local officials were cited. In
Iran one U.S. company reportedly
urged the Shah to purchase a particular model of the F-18 in order to put
pressure on the U.S. Defense department to produce it for the U.S. Navy.
(54)
   (6)Congressional fears that escalating arms sales to Iran and Saudi Arabia were leading to a potentially
dangerous arms race between the two
U.S. surrogates.

Periodic Congressional efforts to introduce
correctives in the U.S. arms program were rarely
successful. Senator Edward Kennedy's proposal
made in 1975 that a moratorium be placed on arms
sales to the Persian Gulf until the administration provided a satisfactory explanation for its
goals and policies in the Gulf was not adopted.
In October 1975, 102 members of Congress from
both parties wrote Secretary Kissinger of their
deep concern about the "anarchic and escalating
nature of the world-wide rush to acquire new
weapons." They asked the government to sponsor an
international conference of arms-exporting nations
to seek "rational control" over an apparent "path-
ological competition in foreign military sales."
(55) Other members of Congress called for "moder-
ating" U.S. sales to the Persian Gulf. None of
these Congressional initiatives produced results
in the executive branch.
      Finally in 1976 Congress passed the important
Arms Export Control Act which the Ford administration accepted with some reservations. Henceforward
all sales of over $25 million in weapons or ancil-
lary services to non-NATO countries were subject
to Congressional scrutiny. A concurrent resolution by both Houses of Congress within a 30-day

period could block a sale. It remained an open question whether Congress, so empowered, would in fact override a Presidential recommendation, if the President's primacy in foreign policymaking were made a public issue.

*Oil Embargoes and the Use of Force*

After the imposition of the Arab oil embargo in 1973-74 Congress as well as the executive branch debated U.S. policy options in case of future interruptions in Middle East oil imports. Should the U.S. rely on collaborative self-help with other oil-consuming countries? Or should the U.S. deploy military troops in the Gulf region to insure a regular flow of oil? If so, in what specific areas should the troops be deployed? How could the U.S. deal with sabotage in the oil fields by a hostile local population? Should the U.S. plan anticipate an indefinite military occupation of the oil fields?

These were among the questions considered in an important Congressional study issued in 1975 regarding U.S. military intervention in the Gulf. (56) The study concluded that U.S. military operations in the Gulf would "combine high costs with high risks," that the prospects for success were poor and the penalty for failure "enormous." Certain criteria were set forth for a successful military operation including the following: (1) seizure of the required oil installations intact; (2) the capacity to secure them for weeks or months, if not years, which would probably require two to four U.S. divisions plus support forces; (3) the operation of all installations without the owner's assistance; and (4) guaranteed safe overseas passage for supplies and petroleum products. Among hypothetical targets a "core area" in Saudi

Arabia covering four onshore oil fields and one offshore producer was preferred.

Possible counteractions by OPEC were canvassed. An unfriendly Iran might mine the chokepoint at the Strait of Hormuz. Local guerillas operating from Omani coves could attack limpet mines on supertankers as they traversed the Strait at night. Even before U.S. landings saboteurs could easily ignite the oil wells. If the infrastructure were in fact wrecked, it would put the source of one-fourth of the world's oil production out of commission for an estimated two years. Direct Soviet intervention was considered a distinct possibility with Soviet submarines in the Gulf posing a serious problem. Some experts argued that foreign intervention in the Gulf oil fields carried the risk of escalation into nuclear war.

– – –

Other Congressional criticisms included the following points: the administration had acquiesced too readily in the cycle of OPEC price increses; the U.S. should make bolder use of its leverage as a major arms supplier to the Gulf area to induce "more reasonable" oil pricing by OPEC; and the U.S. government should have a clearer awareness that an early settlement of the Arab-Israeli conflict was closely linked to a continued flow of Arab oil to the West.

(6) *Summation*

As the Nixon-Ford administrations drew to a close in 1976 the full dimensions of the two-pillar policy in the Persian Gulf were reasonably clear.

Certain of its important features can be summarized as follows:

(1)Heavy reliance on arms transfers as the principal instrument of American influence in the Gulf. The architects of the policy believed these sales would materially advance U.S. interests. As long as the U.S. supplied Gulf oil producers with a wide range of military equipment, there would be no serious interruption of Gulf oil exports. Also arms transactions involving the recycling of petrodollars would relieve the chronic problem of U.S. balance of payments. The Arab oil embargo of 1973-74 had shaken confidence in the first assumption, and the second was subject to the vicissitudes of the world oil market.

(2)A tilted U.S. commitment to preserving a conservative status quo in the Gulf region and marked reluctance to have even formal contacts with challengers to the status quo. Without an apparently conscious decision the U.S. had aligned itself with obsolescent historical forces, i.e. highly traditional sheikdoms of uncertain political tenure.

(3)Substantial technical assistance for ambitious national programs of economic development based on dubiously appropriate Western models. Relevant questions such as the pace of modernization and degree of industrialization tended to be brushed aside by U.S. planners.

(4)The complex role of expatriate cadres of American technicians in several Gulf countries as agents of alien forms of modernization. Would they not in the end become hostages to changing political tides in the region?

(5)A striking dependency of U.S. government programs on American private contractors for full implementation. In Washington these corporate representations were a vested constituency attached to the Pentagon and capable of shaping the costs and specific types of weapons in U.S. arms transfers. In Gulf countries the American contractors were not easily controlled either by U.S. officials or the host country, and in some cases were involved in local corruption.

(6)The recurrence of serious divergent interests between the U.S. and its regional clients despite the complex of shared interests between them. These included disputes over abrupt dislocations in oil supplies and how best to deal with the Palestine question. If divergences persisted would regional surrogates continue to be reliable agents of American interests?

(7)Vulnerability to downgrading in relative importance of U.S. policy priorities as seen during the period Secretary Kissinger was involved in negotiating Arab-Israeli disengagement agreements in 1974-75. In such periods Persian Gulf questions tended to be placed on the "back burner" in Washington.

- - -

With the election of Jimmy Carter in 1976 there was much speculation as to future U.S. policy. Would President Carter retain or radically modify the two-pillar policy? Would he attempt to check the flow of U.S. arms transfers? Would he give more attention to internal practices in Gulf countries? Would he prove flexible in dealing with the Soviet Union and even accept the Soviets as a regional collaborator?

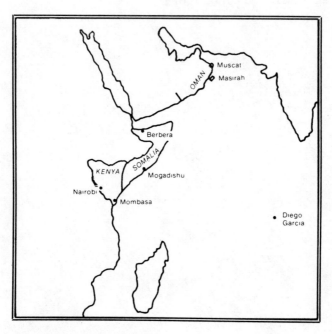

U.S. "ACCESS" FACILITIES
IN THE PERSIAN GULF

## II
## THE CARTER ADMINISTRATION:
## NEW DIRECTIONS IN GULF POLICY

### (1)  *The 1977-78 Period*

Three policy innovations of the Carter administration had direct relevance for the Persian
Gulf.  They were: (1)a new more controlled arms
policy; (2)a highly idealistic human rights campaign, designed to push authoritarian regimes in
a democratic direction; and (3)an exceptionally
determined effort to bring about a final settlement of the Arab-Israeli conflict.

Certain linkages were attempted between these
policies but not always sustained.  These policies
had broad scope and were unevenly applied to Persian Gulf states.  Iran was chiefly affected by
the new arms transfer and human rights policies,
Saudi Arabia and to a lesser extent the Gulf sheikdoms by the arms transfer policy and American peace
effort.

Both during the 1976 Presidential campaign and in the early days of his administration Jimmy Carter made clear his determination to alter the escalating arms sales associated with the Nixon-Ford administrations. The United States accounted for more than half of the annual amount of global arms sales exceeding $20 billion. Between 1950-76 U.S. transfers of arms and related military services were estimated at $110 billion, and military sales in 1976 alone totaled over $9 billion in 68 countries, while unfilled orders were estimated at a further $32 billion.

On May 19, 1977 Carter issued Presidential Directive 13 which set new guidelines for U.S. arms sales.(57) Henceforth arms transfers would be regarded "as an exceptional foreign policy implement," Carter said, used only where it can be clearly demonstrated that the transfer "contribute to our national security interests." The "burden of persuasion" would be placed on those who favored a particular sale rather than those who opposed it. Certain important exceptions were allowed under the new restrictive guidelines including countries with which the U.S. had major defense treaties--NATO, Japan, Australia, and New Zealand. At the behest of the pro-Israel bloc in Congress the administration would take account of "our historic responsibilities to assure the security of the State of Israel." Most importantly of all, "extraordinary circumstances" might necessitate a waiving of some of the new restrictions at Presidential discretion.

The guidelines provided for the following restrictions on future arms transfers. A dollar ceiling would be placed on the volume of new arms commitments with the total for the fiscal year 1978 less than the previous year, to be followed by subsequent annual reductions. The U.S. would not be

the first supplier to introduce into a region like
the Persian Gulf "newly developed, advanced weapons
systems" which would create "significantly higher"
combat capability; here the intent was to discourage intra-regional arms competitions.  The U.S.
would not sell newly developed weapons systems until they had been operationally deployed with U.S.
forces.  The U.S. would not permit co-production
agreements with other states for "significant weapons, equipment, and major components" as these
tended to increase the numbers of arms suppliers.
Nor would the U.S. allow its weapons or equipment
to be transferred to third parties without government consent.  As applied to the Middle East this
guideline was intended in part to allay Israeli
fears as to the ultimate disposition of U.S. arms
shipped to certain Arab states.  U.S. embassy and
military representatives abroad were instructed
not to engage in promotional activities regarding
the sale of conventional arms.

The new arms transfer policy was originally
supposed to be linked to the administration's emphasis on improving human rights in Third World
countries by making future security assistance
programs in some instances conditional on the recipient country's performance record on human
rights.  In the implementation of the new arms
transfer policy two factors served to reduce its
effectiveness: the cumulative momentum in favor
of very large arms sales inherited from past administrations and the complication of political
exigencies that arose in particular cases.

Its application to Iran was a case in point.
The Shah had prepared an extensive shopping list
of U.S. equipment.  This included AWACS planes
(early warning and command systems), an additional
purchase of 140 F-16 aircraft, M-60 tanks, the
F-4G ("wild weasel"), and F-18 aircraft.  In addition the Shah anticipated acquiring special fa-

cilities for co-production of advanced weapons already purchased. The Carter administration's new guidelines were differentially applied to the Shah's multiple requests, which were subjected to both Congressional criticism and divided counsel in the administration. The sale of the 140 F-16s to which the Shah had attached high priority was initially approved in a joint memorandum by the secretaries of Defense and State. But under pressure from several staff members on the National Security Council, Presidential adviser Brzezinski recommended a reduction in the number of F-16s to be sold. The President supported Brzezinski, and the Shah was so informed. Also the F-18 was not sold to Iran because the U.S. military decided not to build it for its own use.

The proposed sale of seven AWACS planes for $1.3 billion was given especially close scrutiny in Congress. Fears were expressed that such highly sensitive advanced equipment might fall into hands "hostile to the U.S." Only after administration assurances regarding the protection or exclusion of certain electronic equipment was the AWACS deal approved. The scheduled delivery date for the AWACS planes was 1981. The Shah's request for a squadron of F-4 "wild weasels" which had sophisticated electronic capabilities engendered another bureaucratic dispute in Washington. The Defense department strongly endorsed the F-4 request, Secretary of State Vance opposed it. In this case the President opted in Vance's favor.

The Defense department, consistently sympathetic to the Shah's arms requests, adopted certain devices which circumvented some of the administration's own guidelines.(58) Iranian orders for specific major items were placed on a multiyear basis, so that Iran would not exceed the arms sale ceiling in any given year. Certain of the major parts of naval frigates ordered by the Shah were built in West Germany, which was not covered by the Carter ceiling.  In summary it can be said that the administration's guidelines on arms sales had limited effect in Iran, and the frequency of bureaucratic clashes over particular items on the Shah's list introduced a recurrent element of uncertainty in their application.  In the case of Saudi Arabia the guidelines were subject to the special requirements of the administration's effort to settle the Arab-Israeli conflict, which will be considered below.

## The Human Rights Campaign

The high priority initially assigned the human rights campaign reflected the tone of moral idealism which typified much of Carter's foreign policy.(59)  The pursuit of idealistic national goals was in part a redemptive process, removing the stain of Watergate scandals from the American image.  Future requests from friendly Third World countries for economic assistance or arms transfers would be weighed against their respective human rights records.  Those countries that resorted to such reprehensible practices as the torture of political prisoners, arbitrary arrest or imprisonment, denial of fair public trial and repression of free speech, press and assembly would be expected to correct these abuses or suffer the loss of American largesse.  To facilitate the implementation of this campaign the State Department published an annual country-by-country survey of their variable records on human rights.

The application of the human rights campaign to Iran proved difficult.  The authoritarian character of the Shah's regime was well-known, but the Shah had previously demonstrated a noteworthy suppleness in countering American criticism.  When

the Kennedy administration exerted pressure on the
Shah in 1961 to liberalize his government, the Shah
made several concessions without seriously weaken-
ing his own power. Even before the advent of the
Carter administration the Shah invited several international agencies to visit Iran in 1976 and sug-
gest ways of improving human rights in Iran.

In 1977 the Shah took several important steps
designed to impress the new administration in Washington. The number of political prisoners jailed
without trial was reduced, and a substantial number were released. Several thousand, however, remained in jail. Some of SAVAK's methods of torture
were said to be eliminated. Under explicit U.S.
pressure the notorious head of SAVAK, General
Nematollah Nassiri, was removed and given an am-
bassadorial appointment. In 1978 additional reforms were introduced including civil court trials
for political offenders. Some critics were skep-
tical that these reforms were anything more than
window-dressing for gullible Americans.

The State Department reports on Iran tended
to rationalize Iran's deficiencies on human rights
by stressing the forced pace of economic and social
modernization and the chronic threat of terrorism
against the government.(60) No serious attempt was
made by the Carter administration to link Iran's
alleged violations of human rights with a reduced
scale of arms transfers to Iran. President Carter
himself appeared inordinately pleased with Iran's
claims of progress in human rights. In his New
Year's day visit to Iran in 1978 Carter praised
Iran as an "island of stability" and lauded the
Shah's leadership and the "admiration and love"
shown the Shah by his people. This Presidential
encomium came almost exactly a year before the
Shah's fall.

Although the immediate focus of the Carter administration's expanded efforts to settle the Arab-
Israeli conflict was logically the "front-line"
states (Egypt, Israel, and Syria) Saudi Arabia also
had a major stake in their outcome. The Saudis
hoped Carter would follow a more even-handed policy
between the two sides than his predecessors and exert increased pressure on the Israelis to withdraw
from the occupied territories. Even before Carter's
inaugural the Saudis took certain steps in antici-
pation of fresh peace moves.(61) They played an
important role in bringing Lebanon's bitter civil
war to a temporary halt and persuaded Egypt and
Syria, hitherto at loggerheads, to cooperate in any
new peace initiative. In OPEC in December Saudi
Arabia supported a moderate increase in oil prices,
partly to encourage the U.S. to adopt a more bal-
anced policy. After assuming office Carter appointed a personal friend, John C. West, former governor
of South Carolina, as ambassador to Saudi Arabia,
assuring the Saudis direct access to the White
House.

By 1977 it was clear that Kissinger's earlier
policy of step-by-step diplomacy had run its
course. As a more viable alternative the Carter
administration embraced the so-called "comprehensive option."(62) This involved the convoking of
the adjourned Geneva conference, eliciting the
cooperation of the Soviets whom Kissinger had shut
out of the peace process and devising a plan for
Palestinian representation that would be accept-
able to the Israelis. In March 1977 at a town
meeting in Clinton, Massachusetts, Carter in a sur-
prising innovative statement referred affirmatively
to a "homeland" for the Palestinians. The Saudis
welcomed the President's new approach. In May
Crown Prince Fahd visited the U.S., and subse-

75

quently the Saudis attempted to induce Yasir Ara-
fat's Palestine Liberation Organization(PLO) to
modify its long-standing refusal to recognize Israel, thus facilitating Palestinian representation
at Geneva.

The mounting expectations of a conclusive
break-through did not materialize. Under heavy
Syrian pressure the PLO declined to accept UN Resolution 242 as a pre-condition for entering into
talks with the U.S. In October 1977 the U.S. and
Soviet Union issued a Joint Communique, calling
for an early resumption of the Geneva conference
but without reference to UN Resolution 242. Influential Congressmen, led by Senator Henry Jackson, harshly attacked the readmission of the Russians to the negotiating process. After Egyptian
President Sadat launched his independent effort to
enter into direct talks with the Israelis by a
dramatic visit to Jerusalem in November 1977, it
became increasingly clear that Carter's comprehensive approach was not a live option. Taken aback
by Sadat's initiative the Saudis decided to mark
time until its consequences for the Arab world became clear.

In the interval the Saudis pressed Washington
for an early decision on its earlier request for
F-15 advanced jet fighters. In view of Saudi Arabia's importance to the ongoing peace process it
became an open question whether the administration's
goal of reducing global arms sales would prevail.
An added complication was that in the last days of
the Ford administration Saudi Arabia had been given
assurances by Secretary Kissinger that Washington
favored the sale of U.S. fighter planes of the
Saudi's own choice.

As in the case of Iran the Saudi arms request
produced a spate of conflicting opinions in official Washington. The Arms Control and Disarmament
agency opposed the sale of F-15s, predicting it

would lead to similar requests from other Middle Eastern countries and hence accelerate arms competition in the region. Spokesmen for the Bureau of political-military affairs in the State Department argued the sale would undermine the new guidelines on arms sales and predicted it would encounter strong opposition in Congress. The President opted in favor of the sale. The Saudis were pointedly making the proposed sale a crucial test of their "special relationship" to the U.S., and Carter was anxious to retain Saudi support for a prospective peace settlement.

To minimize Congressional opposition the administration employed the innovative tactic of combining arms requests from Saudi Arabia and Egypt to match those from Israel in a single "arms package" totalling $4.8 billion. Saudi Arabia would receive 60 F-15s, Egypt 50 F-5 fighter planes, while 75 F-16s and 15 F-15s would be shipped to Israel. The administration further insisted Congress would have to approve all three requests, or the entire package would be withdrawn.

The Congressional fight was bitter. The formidable pro-Israel bloc argued that if Saudi Arabia acquired sophisticated F-15s, Israeli security would be jeopardized. Administration supporters responded that Saudi Arabia had legitimate security needs that arose from its vast area and exposed borders. A rejection by the U.S., it was claimed, would also force the Saudis to turn to other arms suppliers. Offstage the Saudis were deeply involved. They hired professional lobbyists to promote their cause in Washington including a former assistant secretary of state, and sent a number of their younger leaders to argue the Saudi case before Congress and American public opinion. Their articulate oil minister, Sheik Yamani, warned that a refusal to sell the F-15 would adversely affect Saudi oil production policy. On May 15 after an acrimonious Senate debate the arms package was approved by a narrow margin of 55-44. Rarely had the complex linkages between three important strands of U.S. foreign policy--arms sales, oil pricing, and the Middle Eastern peace effort, been so visible in concentrated form.

The presumed gain for Saudi-U.S. relations was qualified, however, by certain concessions the Carter administration felt obliged to make to Congress, which Saudi Arabia reluctantly approved. (63) The Saudis agreed not to purchase bomb racks that enhanced the F-15's offensive capabilities or external fuel tanks that increased their combat radius. Nor would the F-15s be based at Tabuk in northwest Saudi Arabia within range of Israel. Finally no transfer of the F-15s to third states would be allowed by the U.S. The Saudis made no effort to conceal their injured national feelings. Prince Saud, the foreign minister, complained that Saudi Arabia was the only country to have conditions imposed on it.

Fresh strains were introduced in U.S.-Saudi relations by U.S. sponsorship of the Camp David agreement between Israel and Egypt in September 1978. Inexplicably Washington failed to consult with Saudi Arabia in advance. The agreement was comprised of two unrelated parts. The first envisioned a gradual Israeli withdrawal from the Sinai territory Israel had taken over in the 1967 war. The second part dealt inconclusively with the Palestinian question, setting forth a vaguely defined autonomous regime for the occupied West Bank and Gaza. A formal peace treaty was scheduled to be quickly negotiated between Israel and Egypt, terminating 30 years of war in the Middle East.

The initial Saudi reaction to Camp David was equivocal. But at an Arab summit held in Baghdad in November 1978, Saudi Arabia joined the majority

of other Arab states in denouncing Egypt's "separate peace" with the Zionists. The imperatives of
Arab solidarity won out over Saudi reluctance to
undercut continued close relations with the U.S.
Nor could Saudi Arabia fail to consider the threatening prospect of retaliation from radical Arab
states, if the Saudis absented themselves from the
Baghdad sessions. After the signing of the Egyp-
tian-Israel peace treaty in March 1979 Saudi Arabia participated in collective Arab sanctions of a
sweeping character against Egypt. The Carter administration's campaign to attract broadly based
support for its ambitious peace effort among moderate Arabs, led by Saudi Arabia, had ended in
failure.

### (2)  *The 1979-80 Phase*

*The U.S. and the Fall of the Shah*

The Carter administration was slow to recognize the gravity of the developing revolutionary
situation in Iran. It was as late as September
1978 before key policymakers in Washington grasped
the full seriousness of the mass protests against
the Shah's regime. Several factors explain the
lapse. The administration was preoccupied with
the Camp David negotiations which were given the
highest priority. Intelligence reporting was de-
ficient.(64) The American CIA had few contacts
with the Shah's opposition. A CIA assessment
issued in August 1978 stated that "Iran is not in
a revolutionary or even a 'prerevolutionary' situation." A report by the Defense Intelligence
Agency(DIA) concluded that the "shah is expected
to remain in power over the next 10 years." The
Bureau of intelligence and research in the State
Department had no full-time Iran analyst. U.S.

intelligence officials in Iran were said to be
too dependent on SAVAK with its pro-regime bias.
Finally there was a sizable bloc of Carter's advisers, especially among the fervent protagonists
of the human rights campaign, that were either in-
different to the Shah's fate or looked forward to
his political demise.

There was impressive evidence by January 1978
that the revolutionary movement was acquiring ir-
resistible momentum. On January 9--only eight days
after President Carter's visit in Teheran, serious
disturbances broke out in the Shia holy city of
Qum. They were triggered off by a scurrilous press
attack, government-inspired, against the exiled
Ayatollah Khomeini, who was emerging as the single
most important revolutionary leader. The Shah's
police fired on the crowd of demonstrators including many theology students, killing or wounding a
number of people. The revolutionary movement was
by no means exclusively an instrument for Shia
mullahs, who had long been antagonistic to secular-
ist trends in the Shah's modernization program. It
was representative of virtually every major social
group in Iran. Among its diverse supporters were
*bazaari* merchants, opposed to certain of the government's tax policies and the Shah's encouragement of modern supermarkets to replace the traditional *suk*; feudal landowners, hostile to land reforms the Shah had sponsored in his "White Revolution" in the 1960s; university students in large
numbers, deeply opposed to political repression,
especially the activities of SAVAK; an incongruous
admixture of leftist groups ranging from Islamic
militants to the pro-communist Tudeh party. This
heterogeneous coalition was held together by a
shared dislike of the Shah's authoritarianism and
the charismatic personality of the aged Khomeini.
His inflammatory sermons attacking the Shah, re-
corded on casette tapes during his exile in France

and constantly replayed in Iranian mosques, had wide impact and were peculiarily difficult for SAVAK to monitor.

On September 7 there occurred the famous "Black Friday" incident which some writers hold was the decisive turning point in the fortunes of the revolutionary movement. Two days earlier the Iranian ambassador to the U.S., Ardeshir Zahedi, had arrived in Teheran to report to the Shah on his conversations with Presidential adviser Brzezinski, who favored a hard-line stand by the Shah. The Shah decided to ban public demonstrations and impose martial law. An estimated 10,000 persons converged on Jaleh Square in central Teheran in defiance of the government's ban. The Shah's troops fired on the crowd, the estimate of casualties ranging from 700 to 2,000 persons. Riots spread to other Iranian cities.

Washington was now cognizant of the Shah's endangered position. But in the critical days that followed no bureaucratic consensus emerged as to the proper course the President should adopt, and a major debate ensued. The principal antagonists were the staff of the National Security Council (NSC) and high-ranking officials in the State Department. In its distillate form this controversy was personalized in the opposing views of Secretary Vance and Brzezinski. In November a special coordinating committee of the NSC, comprised of Vance, Brzezinski, Defense Secretary Brown, and CIA Director Turner, became the major forum for the disputants but failed to make conclusive findings.

Vance, strongly influenced by advocates of the administration's human rights policy, upheld the position that "the Shah was the problem." As revolutionary violence intensified it appeared increasingly unlikely the Shah could continue to hold power. In Vance's opinion the U.S. should attempt to work with moderate elements in the revolutionary coalition and create a new, more progressive government.  The U.S. would then exert its considerable influence in the armed forces to assure their support for the new government.  In retrospect the position taken by Vance and his faction seriously underestimated the relative strength of the Shia mullahs in the revolutionary coalition and Khomeini's determination to establish a radical Islamic republic.  At that time none of Khomeini's published works was in circulation in Washington.

Brzezinski for his part urged the adoption of strong measures to avert the Shah's fall with its inevitably disruptive effects on the regional balance of power.  If the U.S. failed to give the Shah unequivocal support, U.S. credibility throughout the Middle East would suffer.  In Brzezinski's view it was likely that the Shah would have to resort to the "iron fist" to sustain his position, making internal reforms increasingly irrelevant. Energy Secretary James Schlesinger as a former Defense Secretary and CIA Director lent a powerful voice in support of Brzezinski's position. Schlesinger went one step further, advocating the projection of U.S. military force in the Persian Gulf.  His proposal included strengthening U.S. naval forces in Diego Garcia, deploying aircraft carriers in the area, and stationing significant numbers of Marines close to Iran.  Oddly this was almost the exact course the U.S. followed later in 1979.

President Carter appeared incapable of choosing decisively among these several options.  At times his statements echoed Brzezinski, at other times, Vance.  At one point he appeared to be following Schlesinger's advice when he issued a secret order to move the U.S. carrier *Constellation* from Subic Bay in the Philippines to the Indian Ocean.  But when news of this transfer was leaked by its bureaucratic opponents, Carter ordered the carrier back to Subic Bay. As the Shah's position continued to deteriorate in December, the President reiterated continued U.S. support for the Shah. But the effect of his statements was weakened by an important qualifier that the ultimate decision lay "in the hands of the Iranian people." The impression grew in Iran that the U.S. was preparing to dump the Shah.

The final revolutionary phase was ushered in by the Shah's climactic decision in January 1979 to appoint Shahpour Bakhtiar as the new prime minister. He himself would depart Iran on an extended "vacation." Bakhtiar had been identified with the National Front opposition to the Shah in the 1953 crisis, but his acceptance of the Shah's appointment was repudiated by his own party. The U.S. announced it would support the new Bakhtiar government but would not attempt to influence the Shah either to remain or depart the country. The critical question now became the degree of public support that Bakhtiar could mobilize and what action the armed forces, habitually loyal to the Shah, might take in the still fluid revolutionary situation.

Meanwhile the U.S. Ambassador in Iran, William H. Sullivan, a veteran career diplomat, had been urging—with little guidance from Washington, that the U.S. promote an accommodation between Khomeini's popular forces and the army, once certain senior commanders too closely associated with the Shah had been removed.(65) In Sullivan's view this arrangement would facilitate a relatively smooth governmental changeover, beneficial to U.S. interests. A last-minute arrangement for a high-ranking American representative, Theodore Eliot, the inspector general of the foreign service, to talk with Khomeini in Paris in early January was abruptly cancelled, reportedly because Brzezinski had interceded with the President to prevent it. When Bakhtiar took over as prime minister, Brzezinski supported him and argued that the armed forces could be induced to support Bakhtiar over Khomeini. Later events confirmed Sullivan's views on the irreversibility of the revolution led by Khomeini and the political irrelevance of the French-speaking Bakhtiar.

At this critical juncture President Carter decided to send General Robert Huyser, deputy commander of U.S. military forces in Europe, on a special mission to Iran. His instructions were marked by a certain ambiguity. He was apparently told that he must prevent a military coup as long as the Bakhtiar government had a chance of success, but at the same time must prepare a coup as a "military safety net," should the situation deteriorate. Huyser was in Iran from early January to early February 1979, but his mission, based on a series of talks with high-ranking Iranian officers, had inconclusive results whose significance is still subject to debate. In his reports to Washington Huyser repeatedly inflated Bakhtiar's prospects and the military's willingness to stage a coup if circumstances required it.

Huyser's mission was overtaken by events. Ayatollah Khomeini returned triumphantly to Teheran February 1. He appointed a social democratic moderate, Mehdi Bazargan, to head a rival government to Bakhtiar. Massive street demonstrations continued. The disintegration of the armed forces was set in motion, when Khomeini's guerillas on February 9 routed the imperial guard, long considered Iran's elite force. On February 11 the 26 generals of the Supreme Council of the armed forces issued an unanimous statement that "to avoid bloodshed and chaos the armed forces declare themselves neutral in this political conflict and order their troops to return to their barracks."(66) It was clear that the "military safety net," desired by the U.S., would not be activated. Bakhtiar quickly resigned. The revolutionary forces with which the U.S. had failed to establish meaningful contact, reigned supreme.

For the U.S. the fall-out effects of the Shah's fall were severe. The regional balance of power had been substantially changed to U.S. disadvantage. While the Soviet Union had not made a clear-cut gain, Moscow viewed with satisfaction an obvious setback for its superpower rival. It would require another two years for the U.S. to appreciate the larger significance of Khomeini's advent to power and its destabilizing influence on the whole region. The validity of the two-pillar policy which the U.S. had followed for nearly a decade was now widely discounted. The billions of dollars of arms which the U.S. had poured into Iran since 1971 had in the end proved useless. If regional surrogates were fatally unstable, would not the U.S. in the future have to rely essentially on its own military resources? Finally the indecisiveness of the Carter administration in the Shah's final crisis coupled with what was widely perceived as U.S. "desertion" of an important ally seriously damaged U.S. credibility in the region.


*Steps Toward a New U.S. Policy*


In the aftermath of the Iranian revolution the Carter administration took immediate steps to shore up its weakened position in the Gulf region. Important policy statements by two key officials indicated the U.S. was dropping its non-interventionist stance of the past decade and was prepared to use its own military forces to protect its interests in the Persian Gulf.(67) Defense Secretary Brown stated that "in the protection of those vi-

tal interests"--including the protection of the
oil flow from the Middle East, "we'll take any action that's appropriate, including the use of military force." Reiterating that the U.S. has "vital interests in the Persian Gulf," Energy Secretary Schlesinger insisted that the U.S. "must move
in such a way that it protects those interests,
even if that involves the use of military strength,
of military presence." At the urging of Presidential adviser Brzezinski the Pentagon began to lay
the groundwork for the projection of an American
rapid deployment force to meet future emergency
situations in the region.

Due to the abrupt dissolution of the two-
pillar policy in 1979 the administration gave
special attention to reinvigorating its special
relationship with Saudi Arabia. Saudi anxieties
regarding U.S. policy had increased with the fall
of the Shah and the imminent signature of the
Egyptian-Israeli peace treaty under U.S. auspices.
In February Secretary Brown visited Saudi Arabia
and promised a more active U.S. policy in the region. His offer of an explicit defense arrangement was not accepted partly due to Saudi insistence on prior revisions in the U.S. policy on
Camp David. But Washington did assume in 1979 a
significantly expanded training and advisory function with the Saudi armed forces, including field
and combat maneuvers.(68)

The sudden eruption of war between South
Yemen(PDRY) and North Yemen(YAR) in March 1979
provided the administration with an opportunity
to demonstrate its new receptivity to U.S. military involvement in the larger Gulf region. Once
again the U.S. was essentially acting in support
of Saudi interests. The Saudis perceived South
Yemen's attack on the YAR as a calculated PDRY-
Cuban-Soviet probe to overthrow the relatively
conservative government in the north and test

Saudi and Western reactions. They appealed to the U.S. for immediate assistance to which Washington made a favorable response.

Following Secretary Vance's warning to Moscow against any Soviet-Cuban involvement in the Yemeni war a U.S. naval task force was dispatched to the Arabian Sea. This time the carrier *Constellation* moved in a single direction. On March 9 President Carter invoked for the first time the emergency provisions of the 1976 Arms Export Control Act which authorized the President to initiate arms shipments without the delay of a Congressional review. The delivery to the YAR of $390 million in arms including 12 F-5E aircraft was to be completed within two weeks. The weapons would be shipped first to Saudi Arabia, where they would be assembled and made ready for combat by Saudi and U.S. technicians. Fewer than 100 Americans would be sent to Yemen, and none would be involved, the administration hastened to add, in combat missions. Continued Saudi ambivalence toward the United States was evident, however, when Riyadh decided not to accept the offer of a U.S. F-15 squadron to bolster Saudi air defenses.

The administration's decision to send arms to the YAR provoked considerable Congressional criticism, especially from members of the President's own party.(69) House member Lee Hamilton, chairman of the Foreign Affairs subcommittee on the Near East, questioned the President's recourse to emergency powers in rushing arms to Yemen. His colleague, Lee Aspin, scored the sending of sophisticated weaponry to an army with fewer than 1,000 soldiers who can read and write. Aspin charged the administration was "jumping in because it's the first thing to come along since the decision to change our foreign policy." Congressman Gerry Studds argued that just as in Vietnam and Iran, the U.S. was misinterpreting purely local political problems as superpower showdowns.

The Yemeni war ended on March 17 as abruptly
as it began. A cease-fire was attributed to the
efforts of an Arab League team which visited both
North and South Yemen. Iraq and Syria played a
prominent role in this mediatory effort as did
Saudi Arabia. The Soviet Union, an important military supplier for South Yemen, was obliged to en-
dorse the cease-fire, once its Iraqi and Syrian
clients approved it.

The Carter administration claimed its strong
response in the Yemeni crisis paved the way for a
quick end to the war. In retrospect the U.S. action appeared to be an overreaction to a relatively minor crisis with virtually no payoff for
its costly arms shipments to North Yemen.

*New Crises in the Persian Gulf*

Towards the end of 1979 two separate but in-
terconnected developments propelled the U.S. further in the direction of a "forward" policy in the
Gulf: the seizure of American hostages in Iran in
early November and the Soviet invasion of Afghanistan in late December. There ensued a decided
change in the whole tone of the Carter administration: less emphasis on human rights, "democratiz-
ing" authoritarian regimes overseas and limitations on arms transfers; increased emphasis on
U.S. defense expenditures and a systematic effort
to enlarge significantly the U.S. military presence in the Persian Gulf. Only a residual element
of the previous detente policy with the Soviet Union remained.

In the period immediately following the Iranian revolution the U.S. pursued a cautious policy,
striving to salvage whatever possible from the collapse of the Pahlavi regime. It was deemed advis-
able for the U.S. to show a less conspicuous presence. The U.S. military advisory group was reduced

from approximately 400 to six members. Six intelligence gathering bases run by U.S. agencies were closed. Eleven billion dollars worth of arms ordered by the Shah were cancelled by Iran. U.S. diplomatic personnel in Iran avoided provocative statements, moderated their critical comments on violations of human rights, and indicated discreet support for moderate elements in the Bazargan government which had succeeded Bakhtiar. Due to Iran's continued need for spare parts for U.S.-supplied military equipment and additional training of technical specialists, the U.S. maintained a precarious military link with Iran. But an improved U.S. position depended on a strengthening of the moderate forces. The reverse occurred. The relative power position of the Islamic religious elements steadily expanded, the anti-Western xenophobic tone in Iranian political discourse was intense, and a showdown between the U.S., portrayed as the "Great Satan" in world affairs, and the Khomeini forces seemed inevitable.

In late October 1979 the Carter administration reversed its earlier decision not to allow the Shah to establish residence in the U.S. His entry was now approved at the behest of such influential friends as Henry Kissinger and David Rockefeller to enable the Shah to receive specialist medical care. On November 4 an armed group of pro-Khomeini militants invaded the U.S. embassy in Teheran and took about 60 Americans, mostly diplomatic personnel, as hostages. This action was quickly approved by Ayatollah Khomeini, who supported the militants' position that the hostages would be released only if the Shah were returned to Iran to stand trial for his alleged crimes. This was coupled with a demand for a formal American apology for U.S. "crimes" in Iran. In this crisis the relatively moderate Bazargan government was dismissed by the Ayatollah, and the rightist drift in the Iranian government continued.

President Carter, fearing that aggressive action against Iran could jeopardize the lives of the hostages, initially adopted a policy of restraint. In a graduated series of non-military punitive measures Carter took the following steps: (1)ordered a freeze of Iranian assets in the U.S., estimated at between eight and nine billion dollars; (2)asked American companies to stop buying Iranian oil for the U.S. market and exerted pressure on U.S. allies including Japan not to increase their purchases from Iran; (3)assigned two carrier task forces to the Arabian Sea; (4)cancelled over a half billion dollars in shipments of spare parts and terminated most of the training programs of Iranian personnel in the U.S. Supportive United Nations resolutions were passed calling for release of the hostages. In December the President asked the U.N. to impose collective economic sanctions against Iran, which were vetoed by the Soviet Union. The U.S. later broke diplomatic relations with Iran.

On April 24, 1980 the U.S. launched its ill-fated rescue mission to free the hostages. The secret plan was to transport a force of some 200 men by helicopters who would proceed to the embassy in Teheran, overpower the militants, and remove the hostages. When several helicopters encountered mechanical failure the mission was aborted. In the evacuation eight lives were lost. In the Muslim Middle East this U.S. recourse to force was widely castigated. The American rescue mission was formally condemned by 42 foreign ministers at a meeting of the Islamic Conference. American prestige suffered another serious blow, and moderate Arab governments in the Gulf region entertained fresh doubts regarding a U.S. connection.

In Washington five days prior to the rescue attempt Secretary Vance handed in his resignation.

The final decision to go ahead with the rescue plan
was reached April 11 at a meeting of the National
Security Council, when Vance was absent.  Later
Vance warned the President that recourse to force
in Iran would endanger the lives of the hostages,
lower U.S. prestige in the Muslim world, divide
the U.S. from its European allies, and deflect attention from the Soviet Union.

- - -

The background to the Soviet invasion of Afghanistan in December 1979 was complex.  In April
1978 a Marxist military coup in Kabul undertaken
by officers trained in the Soviet Union over the
preceding two decades, led to the creation of the
first Marxist state in Afghanistan, strongly supported by the Soviets.  Bearing the name People's
Democratic Party of Afghanistan(PDPA), the Afghan
Marxists attempted to impose a program of rapid
communization on an illiterate tribal society,
which provoked armed resistance from Afghan tribes-
men and civil war.  The PDPA had long been bedeviled
by severe factionalism, the two major rivals being
the Khalq and the Parcham groups.  After the April
coup the Khalq faction, led by President Nur Mohammed Taraki and his strongman, Hafizullah Amin was
clearly dominant.  The leader of the Parcham faction, Babrak Karmal, was sent into diplomatic exile in Czechoslovakia.  Amin instituted a sweeping
party purge in which hundreds of party members were
killed or imprisoned.  Army morale was severely
damaged by Amin's purges and continued resistance
from tribal rebels.  For the Kremlin the immediate
question was whether the Soviets could afford to
allow their Afghan client to slip into chaos.  In
late December 1979 the Russians moved 50,000 troops
into Afghanistan, later increased to 85,000.  At
Soviet direction the discredited Amin was assasin-

ated and the leader of the Parcham faction, Karmal, was airlifted back to Kabul to head the new Soviet puppet regime.

Divergent interpretations of Soviet motivations were given. Russian charges of American-financed "counter-revolutionary" groups being trained in Pakistan were discounted as self-serving. American proponents of the globalist school, pointing to earlier Soviet support for Marxist regimes in Angola and Ethiopia, argued that the invasion of Afghanistan was yet another installment in a grand Soviet design of imperial expansion. New Soviet bases in Afghanistan would enable the Russians to mount future challenges against neighboring Pakistan and Iran. Western oil sources in the Gulf could now be more easily placed under seige. Other observers stressed the defensive aspects of the Soviet action. The Russians had little choice, it was said, except to discipline their unstable Afghan client and discourage the spread of Islamic fundamentalism, now ascendant in Iran, to Muslim peoples in Soviet republics.

The Carter administration clearly accepted the more negative interpretation of Soviet intent. The Soviet invasion was considered by the administration the most ominous development since World War II, the Russians having sent their own troops for the first time outside eastern Europe. The Soviets had also taken advantage, it was said, of U.S. preoccupation with the hostage crisis in Iran. Somewhat naively President Carter claimed to have received an almost overnight education in the true character of the Soviet regime.

Carter adopted a wide range of policy responses to the Soviet invasion. The U.N. Security met at U.S. initiative, and a resolution co-sponsored by five Third World members of the Council condemned Soviet military intervention in Afghanistan. Convoked in special emergency session the

General Assembly passed a similar resolution by a lop-sided vote 104 to 18 with 18 abstentions. The Soviets were supported only by their own bloc and a few other states, including South Yemen in the Gulf region. Even Iraq with whom the Soviets had a treaty relationship voted to condemn the Soviet Union.

The Carter administration unilaterally took a series of punitive measures against the Soviets for which it tried to enlist the support of its NATO allies. Their response proved disappointing. The effect of the U.S. grain embargo was offset by Soviet imports from other countries. The attempt to restrict high-technology exports to the USSR was undercut by countries like West Germany and France, who wanted to sustain their improved trade relations with the Russians; detente remained an attractive option to many Europeans. While the U.S. gained some support for its boycott of the summer Olympic games in Moscow, several Western states sent teams to Moscow.

Obviously there was no allied consensus on an effective plan to counter the Soviets. Despite the greater reliance of Western Europe on Middle East oil these states were unwilling to increase their defense expenditures significantly to prepare for a military showdown with the Soviet Union in the remote Gulf region. U.S. policy in the Gulf was widely regarded in Europe as erratic and impulsively reactive to passing crises. As the U.S. and its allies quibbled the Soviets consolidated their hold on Afghanistan.

— — —

An integral part of the U.S. reaction to the Soviet invasion was its concentrated effort to bolster the now precarious position of Pakistan. Some U.S. policymakers feared the Soviet Union might make a military thrust across the Khyber Pass. The ultimate Russian goal was assessed as the acquisition of a warm-water port on the Arabian Sea.

Recent U.S.-Pakistan relations had seriously deteriorated. In 1977 a military coup under General Zia ul-Huq led to the establishment of a politically repressive regime. World reaction to the execution of former president Bhutto was sharply negative. In April 1979 the Carter administration cut off all aid to Pakistan as the result of its alleged development of nuclear weapons. Here the administration was acting in compliance with the Symington amendment to the Foreign Assistance Act, which bars aid to countries believed to be engaged in the manufacture of nuclear weapons. Pakistan insisted that its nuclear program was exclusively for peaceful purposes. In November 1979 the U.S. embassy in Islamabad was sacked and burned to the ground by a mob of Islamic extremists. Reportedly they had acted on the basis of a false report that the U.S. was involved in the recent attack on the Grand Mosque in the holy city of Mecca. President Zia's forces had been slow in dispersing the mob, adding fresh strains to U.S. relations with Pakistan.

The Carter administration moved quickly to bring about radically improved relations with Pakistan.(70) The Pakistani foreign minister was invited to Washington for preliminary talks, and the U.S. publicly announced an offer of $400 million in military and economic aid to Pakistan. President Zia contemptuously dismissed this offer as "peanuts" compared to the two or three billion dollars he said was required to rebuild Pakistan's army and economy. The administration was also willing to allay Pakistan's anxieties by reaffirming their 1959 executive agreement, which called for mutual consultation in emergencies. The Zia government wanted more explicit assurances backed up by U.S. weaponry.

Early in February Presidential adviser Brzezinski and the deputy secretary of state, Warren
Christopher, went to Pakistan to establish closer
relations.  During an interval in the talks Brzezinski made a bravura gesture when he visited the
Khyber Pass, where he was photographed brandishing
a rifle in the direction of Afghanistan and the Soviet Union.  In the USSR Soviet propagandists made
effective use of this incident in depicting the
U.S. as a blatant aggressor.  The special U.S.
mission to Pakistan failed to make progress. Pakistan moved to strengthen its ties with the non-
aligned movement.


*The Carter Doctrine*

Since 1947 it has become almost a commonplace
of U.S. foreign policy to attach the pretentious
label of Presidential "doctrine" to major policy
innovations.  Such was the case with a key passage
in President Carter's State of the Union message
in January 1980, quickly dubbed the "Carter Doctrine" by the press.  In a definitive statement of
U.S. policy to meet the strategic threat posed by
the Soviet invasion of Afghanistan, Carter com-
mented as follows:

> Let our position be absolutely clear:
> Any attempt by any outside force to
> gain control of the Persian Gulf re-
> gion will be regarded as an assault on
> vital interests of the United States
> of America, and such an assault will
> be repelled by any means necessary, in-
> cluding military force.(71)

Certain comparisons with earlier Presidential
doctrines applicable to the Middle East are ap-

propriate here. In March 1947 the Truman Doctrine pledged "support for free peoples who are resisting attempted subjugation by armed minorities and outside pressure."(72) Though stated in universalist terms Truman's statement applied initially to crisis situations confronting Greece and Turkey for which the U.S. held the Soviet Union responsible. In this instance U.S. involvement was limited to a $400 million program of military and economic assistance supplemented by the dispatch of a relatively small number of American military and civilian personnel to the eastern Mediterranean.

A clearer precedent was the Eisenhower Doctrine, enunciated in January 1957.(73) Eisenhower's statement was directed to Middle East countries that might fall prey to the machinations of "international communism." The U.S., Eisenhower declared, would employ its armed forces "to secure and protect the territorial integrity and political independence of nations requesting such aid against overt armed aggression from any nation controlled by international communism." At that time Nasserite Egypt with its close connections with the Soviet Union was seen in Washington as a stalking horse for Soviet communism. Even before the Eisenhower Doctrine was formulated the President had declared in November 1956 that the U.S. would view "with utmost gravity" threats to "the territorial integrity or political independence of Persia, Iraq, Pakistan or Turkey."

The single application of the Eisenhower Doctrine was the U.S. decision to send a Marine contingent in May 1958 to bolster the beleagured pro-Western Lebanese government of President Chamoun. In requesting American assistance Chamoun charged that civil disturbances in Lebanon were fomented by Nasser's Egypt. In this instance U.S. Marines landed on the beaches at Beirut without opposition.

But two months later in July the U.S. was unable to prevent the overthrow of the pro-Western government in oil-rich Iraq. Considering Iraq's importance in the U.S.-sponsored Baghdad Pact, this was a major setback to American interests.

The political context in which the Carter Doctrine was launched differed strikingly from that of the Eisenhower Doctrine. In the 1950s the U.S. still enjoyed nuclear superiority over the Soviet Union, and Middle Eastern oil production was still controlled by international oil companies in which American companies played a key role. By the 1980s the overall power position of the U.S. was considerably less favorable. The U.S. now shared nuclear parity with the Soviet Union with some observers claiming the Soviets had forged ahead in nuclear competition. Basic decisions on oil pricing and production levels were now made by OPEC, a powerful cartel whose decisions were only marginally subject to U.S. influence. The once formidable global network of alliances under U.S. direction was in process of disintegration. As a result of the loss of the Vietnam War, American public opinion was subject to strong neo-isolationist pressures. President Carter himself acknowledged that U.S. resources alone were insufficient to cope with future challenges to Western interests in the Gulf region.

Finally the Carter Doctrine stands in partial contrast to the Nixon Doctrine of the 1970s. Under the latter regional surrogates were supposed to defend American interests, and oil-rich recipients of U.S. arms transfers were able to finance their own weaponry. The Carter Doctrine required considerably increased U.S. defense expenditures and primary reliance on America's own military power. But in their mutual preoccupation with anti-Soviet regional power balances and their shared militarist approach to regional security the Nixon and Carter doctrines were coordinates.

From the outset it was apparent the practical application of the Carter Doctrine depended on U.S. capability to project substantial military power in the Gulf region with maximum speed. Formidable obstacles confronted U.S. defense planners. Airline routes from the east coast of the U.S. to the Gulf exceeded 7,000 nautical miles. Sealane routes from the U.S. ranged from 8,500 nautical miles via the Suez Canal, 12,000 nautical miles through the Cape of Good Hope. With the dissolution of CENTO the U.S. no longer had a framework of treaty relationships to facilitate joint contingency planning with local states. The powerful force of Arab nationalism precluded the possibility of permanent U.S. military bases in the region. There were competing demands on U.S. military resources in Europe and East Asia, which would become especially acute, should a crisis in the Gulf coincide with a crisis in either of the other two areas. By contrast the Soviets enjoyed several advantages as follows: the proximity of their long and well-fortified border with Iran from which they could launch a devastating military offensive; the new factor of Soviet air bases in nearby Afghanistan; access to military facilities in South Yemen; and the Soviets' lop-sided advantage in military manpower and range of weaponry which could be quickly injected into a future Gulf showdown.

Administration planning for some kind of rapid deployment force had begun as early as August 1977. At Brzezinski's urging President Carter issued Presidential Review Memorandum 10 which set the planning process in motion. But it was not until December 1979 that Marine Corps General Paul X. Kelley was designated to head the new Rapid Deployment Force(RDF) and March 1980 when the RDF Joint Task Force was established. Several factors contributed to this delay: inter-service rivalries, especially between the Army and Marine Corps; some doubt within the defense establishment itself as to the feasibility of such a force; and the lack of a major crisis until 1979 to stimulate an aggressive campaign for increased defense expenditures which so costly a force required.

In General Kelley's view the RDF was designed to meet the need for a sharper U.S. focus in the Third World before "we let it slip through our fingers."(74) At Senate hearings he defined the purpose of the RDF "to jointly train and exercise" designated forces in the four U.S. services (Army, Navy, Air Force and Marine Corps) and "ultimately employ them in response to contingencies threatening U.S. interests anywhere in the world."(75) It was clear that the likeliest use of the RDF in the near term was the volatile Persian Gulf region.

The "designated forces" for initial participation in the RDF included several Air Force tactical fighter squadrons, four Army divisions of which the most important were the 82nd and 101st Airborne divisions, selected Marine Corps units, and assorted combat support units. The total manpower associated with RDF units was expected to reach 200,000 with an additional 100,000 reservists that would have to be called up to support them.(76) Headquarters for the RDF was set up in the continental U.S. at McDill Air Base in Florida.

The immediate RDF budget commitment in fiscal 1981 was $220 million for the first two of a fleet of "floating bases" and $81 million for developing suitably large transport planes. Over a five-year period an appropriation of approximately $10 billion was anticipated, including $6 billion for airlift capabilities and $3 billion for additional "floating bases." Due to the inflationary factor and the Pentagon's tendency to accumulate cost overruns, the total expenditures by 1986 was likely to be substantially above $10 billion.

Defense Secretary Brown like Brzezinski was an enthusiastic supporter of RDF, and in 1980 he became the chief official spokesman on its behalf. The RDF was officially conceived as a deterrent force to discourage future acts of Soviet aggression in key areas like the Persian Gulf. If it were actually employed, the RDF would presumably perform a "trip wire" function until other military options could be exercised. But Brown denied that in such a contingency the U.S. either "by preference or necessity" would quickly resort to "theater nuclear weapons." Conventional deterrence and defense would suffice in such emergencies.(77)

It was clear, however, that the RDF was not exclusively a deterrent force and could be utilized in preemptive strikes. Brown's own stipulations were as follows:

> It is not necessary for our initial units to be able to defeat the whole force an adversary might eventually have in place. It is also not necessary for us to await the firing of the first shot or the prior arrival of hostile forces; many of our forces can be moved upon strategic warning and some upon receipt of even *very early and ambiguous indications*.(78)

The ultimate effectiveness of the RDF was seen to rest on skillful integration of several key ingredients. First an immediately enlarged U.S. naval presence both in the Gulf region and contiguous areas was ordered. This included adding two destroyers to the small MIDEASTFOR in Bahrain and expanding naval facilities at Diego Garcia in the Indian Ocean to accommodate two aircraft-carrier battle groups with full complements of fighter, antisubmarine and reconnaissance aircraft and an assault team of Marines. Prepositioning of equipment was also seen as vitally important. Early in 1980 a seven-ship force of commercial-type vessels was assembled, loaded with equipment, supplies, fuel and water that would enable a Marine amphibious brigade of some 10,000 men and several Air Force fighter squadrons to operate until logistic support arrived from the U.S. This force was reportedly located within a few days sailing distance from the Persian Gulf-Arabian Sea region.

High priority was accorded the organization of highly mobile air and sealift capabilities. The immediate goal was to insure the arrival of the first battalion of the 82nd Airborne Division in the Gulf region within 48 hours of a movement order, with the entire division being in place within two weeks. Special attention was given to the procurement of aerial tankers and very large "CX" transport aircraft for deployment of outsized cargo like battle tanks.

Frequent exercises by RDF units were scheduled, joined by military units of friendly nations. In 1979 one of the U.S. carrier battle groups conducted an Indian Ocean exercise with naval units from Britain and Australia. In the summer of 1980 an intensive air combat exercise under the code name of "Proud Phantom" was carried out in Egypt by U.S. fighter squadrons in cooperation with an Egyptian Air Force squadron. In a logistical exercise held in November 1980 a battalion of the U.S. Army's 101st Airborne Division and an Air Force detachment were airlifted to Egypt.

A critically important element in the RDF "mix" was negotiation of access agreements with strategically located regional states which provided for use of certain local facilities by U.S. forces in emergency situations. After hard bargaining U.S. access agreements were made in 1980

with Oman in the Gulf region and with Kenya and
Somalia in the Horn of Africa. Without such access future RDF deployments would be virtually
impossible. Certain details of these agreements
are treated in the section below.

The RDF concept was subjected to considerable
criticism both in Congress and by outside experts.
Senator Mark Hatfield supported by House colleagues
argued that an interventionary force would "raise
tensions in the area, jeopardize both the diplomacy
of the region and the availability of its oil and,
perhaps most importantly, critically undermine the
credibility of the United States as peacemaker."
(79) Senator Henry Jackson, a long-time hardliner
on defense issues, questioned whether it was wise
"to lay down a doctrine when there is serious doubt
whether it can be upheld."(80) The utility of the
RDF in protecting Gulf oil fields from sabotage
and political disturbances was also questioned.
Congress cut the original $81 million request for
big CX transport planes to $35 million and made
the funds conditional on completion of preliminary
studies of its feasibility.

*U.S. Access Agreements*

The three access agreements completed in 1980
represented very limited strategic gains for the
U.S. for which Washington made pledges of substantial military and economic assistance.(81) Actual
use of these facilities by the U.S. was subject
to review by the governments concerned when specific crisis situations arose.

The most important of the three agreements
was that made with the Sultanate of Oman due to
its proximity to the Strait of Hormuz. The U.S.
gained increased access to the airstrip on Masirah
island in the Arabian Sea, port facilities in Mus-

cat and limited access to several other airfields. In return Oman was granted military assistance estimated at $100 million. Some critics argued that by implication the agreement with Oman involved U.S. underwriting of the Sultan's personal regime.

The negotiation of agreements with Kenya and Somalia in East Africa was complicated by tensions between the two states, partly due to Somalian claims to territory in northeast Kenya. In June 1980 Kenya granted the U.S. increased use of port facilities at Mombasa, which was already a regular port of call for the U.S. Navy, and use of certain airfields. The U.S. provided Kenya $44 million in military assistance and also food shipments. But in July when the U.S. asked to carry out a small military exercise involving 1,800 men, Kenya refused. Relations with the U.S. were further strained in August when the U.S. signed an access agreement with neighboring Somalia.

The agreement with Somalia granted the U.S. use of air and naval facilities at Berbera, previously available to the Soviet Navy, and at Mogadishu. The U.S. pledged $40 million in military aid over two years and a further $125 million in non-military credits. The agreement with Somalia was criticized by the Marxist Ethiopian government on grounds it would strengthen the Somalian position in the bitter conflict between the two states over the Ogaden region of Ethiopia. In the U.S. Congress similar criticism was voiced. Fears were expressed that the U.S. would be drawn into conflict with the Soviet Union due to the latter's close ties to Ethiopia.

In addition a special arrangement with President Sadat of Egypt granted the U.S. limited use of Ras Banas, located on the Red Sea across from Saudi Arabia, for RDF planes and troops in periods of acute Middle East tension. The U.S. was required to expend between $200 and $400 million to upgrade the Ras Banas facilities.

The gravest weakness of these several agreements was that they might become inoperative in critical emergencies due to changing political circumstances and the local emergence of anti-Western leaders. The U.S. also risked becoming embroiled in the complicated skein of regional politics in East Africa.

*The Iran-Iraq War*

In its initial formulation the Carter Doctrine was directed against any "outside force" that might threaten vital U.S. interests in the Gulf, especially the continued oil flow. Speculation arose regarding a U.S. response to an intra-regional conflict which threatened to interrupt the oil flow or adversely affect the regional balance of power. The outbreak of war between Iran and Iraq in September 1980 provided a test case. Without diplomatic representation in either state the U.S. had limited leverage. Washington feared the protagonists would launch strikes against each other's oil wells and that the choke-point at the Strait of Hormuz might be closed off. In such an eventuality would the U.S. intervene under the Carter Doctrine to protect U.S. interests?

Just prior to the war Iran and Iraq together were exporting approximately four million bpd. (barrels per day). Three American allies were major importers of Iraqi oil: France (24 percent of its total imports), Australia (14 percent), and Japan (10 percent). By the end of 1980 neither Iran nor Iraq were exporting appreciable amounts of oil. In OPEC a big surge in oil prices occurred immediately. The imminent crisis proved less dire than expected. World oil stocks were at an all-time high, and after the war began Saudi Arabia increased its oil production of 9.5 million bpd. by nearly one million bpd.

The war was preceded by nearly a year of border skirmishes between the two states. Iran's Islamic Republic, inspired by the fiery Khomeini, was bent on exporting its revolution into neighboring Arab states. The estimated seven million Iraqi Shias, located mostly in the southern provinces contiguous to Iran, were an important target. The two Shia holy cities, Karbala and Najaf, were located close to the Iraqi capital of Baghdad. The Ayatollah himself had lived nearly a decade and a half in Najaf, from where he had been expelled to France in 1978, at the Shah's insistence.

Iraq had certain grievances against Iran. Not only was Iran fomenting revolution against the secular Baathist government, Iraq was also deeply dissatisfied with the 1975 agreement with Iran in their border dispute over the Shatt al-Arab estuary, over which Iraq now sought full control. A compelling motive for resort to force was Iraqi President Saddam Hussein's perceived determination to make Iraq the hegemonic power in the Persian Gulf and replace renegade Egypt as leader of the Arab world. In 1980 Iran's presumed post-revolutionary weakness and evidence of internal chaos in Teheran emboldened President Hussein to act. Iraq's early gains in the war foreshadowed an Iraqi takeover of the oil-rich Khuzistan province.

Iraq's expectations of an easy military victory were not realized. The Iraqi aggression aroused an intensely nationalist response in Iran enabling the embattled Iranian government to exploit the patriotic war of national defense for purposes of a much-needed national unity. By December the war had stalemated.

At the outset the U.S. was apprehensive that the Soviet Union would intervene in the war and radically improve its power position in the Gulf

region. The Soviets were in turn uncertain of
American reaction if the war caused an actual interruption in the Western oil flow. The new U.S.
Secretary of State, Edmund Muskie, met September
25 with Soviet Foreign Minister Andrei Gromyko,
and both superpowers promised to adhere to a
strict policy of neutrality in the Iran-Iraq war.
To the U.S. a neutral stance seemed the likeliest
option to avoid too gross a disturbance in the existing regional balance.

Early in the war the U.S. was compelled to
consider measures to protect the interests of two
of its closest Gulf associates, Saudi Arabia and
Oman. Intelligence reports were received in Washington that Iraqi helicopters were preparing to
commandeer facilities in Oman and Saudi Arabia in
order to attack Iranian bases across the Gulf as
well as Iranian installations on three Gulf
islands. The Saudis signaled Washington they expected prompt military help from the U.S.

In Washington Brzezinski and Muskie with
their respective advisers debated the form of U.S.
assistance to Saudi Arabia.(82) The Brzezinski
group favored an exceptionally strong U.S. response, including the dispatch of two F-14 squadrons from the U.S. carrier force in the Arabian
Sea matched by an equal number of F-15s from U.S.
bases. This action, it was argued, would lend
credibility to the Carter Doctrine. The Muskie
group on the other hand advocated a more modest
U.S. response in order not to violate the pledge
of neutrality which Muskie had made the Russians.
The administration decided to send four AWACS
planes to Saudi Arabia which had only defensive
capabilities and could be used to plot out a possible Iranian attack.

As the war dragged on the formal neutrality
to which both superpowers were committed was modified. Interestingly both the USSR and the U.S.

for separate reasons "tilted" in favor of Iran over Iraq. Despite its treaty relationship with Iraq the Soviet Union wanted to keep its options open, for Iran was clearly the bigger strategic prize. The Soviets furnished their Iraqi client with limited quantities of spare parts and some civilian supplies. At the same time the Russians strove to maintain friendly relations with Iran's Islamic Republic and arranged for shipment of some military supplies.

The U.S. "tilt" toward Iran had a different context. Washington feared that if Iraq in fact absorbed Khuzistan, heavily populated by Arabs, this would encourage ongoing revolts of other minorities and lead to the dismemberment of Iran. In that eventuality the Soviets could scarcely be expected to stand aside. In October 1980 Secretary Muskie made public reference in unneutral language to Iraq's "invasion" of Iran. President Carter called for a "strong" Iran. It remained to be seen if U.S. warnings against Iran's "dismemberment" would be restricted to verbal protests.

The U.S. then attempted to increase its tilt toward Iran by linking it to the still unresolved hostage issue. This took the form of a U.S. offer to Iran to resume its role as chief military supplier, if the hostage issue were satisfactorily settled. At one point Washington published an impressive list of spare parts the U.S. was willing to ship Iran. Interestingly Iran resisted the overtures of both superpowers. Compared to the U.S. the Soviet Union was a "Lesser Satan," but still not fit company for Islamic purists.

Thus the Iran-Iraq war did not provide a conclusive test for the extension of the Carter Doctrine to intra-regional conflicts. The U.S. had to balance its role of self-appointed protector of Gulf states under seige against too radical an impairment of its relations with Moscow. In any case the U.S. appeared to have an exceptionally narrow range for its requisite maneuverings in the Iran-Iraq war.

*Carter's "Forward" Policy: A Summation*

The Carter administration's foreign policy provided an illuminating example of the limitations of moral idealism as the primary standard of U.S. decision making. Certainly a plausible defense at least in the abstract was possible in the case of three of Carter's initial policies applicable to the Gulf. As cited above these were reversing the escalation in the mid-1970s of the superpower arms sales to Third World countries, linking U.S. assistance programs to critical annual reviews of the recipients' performance in human rights, and sponsoring a vigorous peace-making effort to end the 30 years war in the Middle East. But repeatedly the implementation of these policies led to pragmatic adjustments to the stubborn realities of local situations, and in some instances they were simply inoperative. U.S. arms shipments to Iran remained at high levels during 1977-78 despite continued violations of human rights by the Shah's regime. Carter's serious commitment in 1977 to the so-called "comprehensive option" involving the Soviet Union in settling the Arab-Israeli conflict was scuttled in face of strong Congressional criticism and Israeli resistance. A contributory factor to this pattern of policy shifts was Carter's tendency "to cut and run" when faced with formidable opposition to even his high-priority objectives. The double crisis in 1979 of the fall of the Shah and the Soviet invasion of Afghanistan lowered even further the administration's tone of high idealism. Henceforward there occurred an ineluctable shift to a kind of hesitant *Realpolitik*. The leading spokesmen for this approach among the President's advisers were Brzezinski, Brown, and Schlesinger.

The adoption of an assertive "forward" policy in the Persian Gulf in 1979-80 had multiple consequences, some being debatably in the American interest. The most serious was the return to the cold war with the Soviet Union, carrying the risk of a "final" military showdown between the two superpowers. Increasingly primary attention was given to frequently reiterated public warnings to the Soviets of the dire fate which their future acts of aggression would suffer; a cluster of punitive measures intended to deter Soviet adventurism, most of which the Russians were able to circumvent; and very substantial increases in U.S. defense expenditures, designed especially to enhance the mobility and striking power of U.S. military units in southwest Asia. In the eyes of the Carter administration these boldly conceived measures carried several advantages. Not only would they improve the American image abroad and correct the wide-spread impression that since Vietnam the U.S. had been in a state of rapid decline as a formidable world power. They would also reassure a number of Gulf states that in a serious crisis, they could rely on firm U.S. support. The equivocal U.S. stance in Iran in 1978-79 would not be repeated. Inside the U.S. the new "forward" policy was expected to assuage wounded national pride over Vietnam and stimulate fresh outpourings of patriotic sentiment. Not least of the anticipated gains was that Carter himself would look more "presidential," presumably enhancing his prospects for reelection in 1980.

As the "forward" policy unfolded in the last two years of the Carter administration a number of its shortcomings became evident. Some of the more important of these can be summarized as follows:

(1) The thinness of its conceptualization in the form of the Carter Doctrine. Future U.S. policy in the Gulf appeared to rest essentially on sheer quantitative amassing of U.S. military power. Would this not result in a serious downgrading in the relative importance of U.S. diplomatic contacts in the area which were traditionally utilized for non-violent resolution of regional disputes?

(2) Its dependency on close cooperation between the U.S. and its European allies as well as certain key Gulf states, which in both cases failed to materialize in 1980. Inside NATO the European states appeared unwilling to increase their own military contribution significantly to enable the U.S. to shift some of its European units to the Persian Gulf in future crises. In the Gulf despite strenuous efforts the U.S. was unable to acquire permanent military bases, and only Oman was willing to grant highly conditional access rights to U.S. forces.

(3) Widespread doubts both in the U.S. and in Gulf states that the RDF would prove an effective instrument of the "forward" policy. If its full complement could not be assembled before the middle or late 1980s, would the Soviet Union intervene militarily in the interim period? Considering the formidable advantages of Soviet proximity to the Gulf and its obvious regional military superiority, would even an expanded RDF represent more

than token opposition to a Soviet attack?  If that were the case, did the U.S. position in the Gulf rest ultimately on the nuclear deterrent?  If the U.S. decided to resort to tactical nuclear weapons in the Gulf would a Gulf war spread either to the European theater or to a direct U.S.-Soviet nuclear exchange or both?  With the RDF's heavy reliance on naval task forces was it not vulnerable to attack by Soviet nuclear submarines in the Indian Ocean, and if so, would this lead to a similar escalatory process?

(4) The dubious appropriateness of the "forward" policy in coping with the major internal threat to regional stability--the further spread of Iran's branch of Shia fundamentalism, made more likely by Iran's apparent victory in the war with Iraq.  The combination of the seizure of the mosque in Mecca by a Saudi variant of Islamic militants in November 1979, the subsequent Shia riots in Saudi Arabia's Hasa province, and the abortive Shia coup in Bahrain in December 1981 was an ominous portent for future stability in the Gulf.  The only apparent U.S. answer to this Islamic challenge thus far was continued importation of high technology to bolster development plans in friendly Gulf countries and occasional verbal attempts by U.S. officials to minimize the cultural distance between Muslim societies and Western secular states.  Could the alternative of

large-scale Western military intervention thwart the Islamic revolution in the long term?

Ronald Reagan's election as President in November 1980 raised once again speculation as to
future U.S. policy in the Gulf. Did the advent of
a Republican president foreshadow discontinuities
in U.S. policy there? Would Carter's "forward"
policy be sustained or even extended? Would the
growing tensions of the new cold war with the Soviet Union be further magnified and create new
risks of a military showdown between the superpowers in the Persian Gulf?

# III
## The Reagan Administration's
## Gulf Policy

In the 1980 presidential campaign President Carter's belated conversion to an activist foreign policy in Southwest Asia, his shelving of certain moral imperatives in the interests of national security, and his pledge to bolster American military power by an annual 5 percent increase in defense expenditures proved unavailing. His past indecisiveness, the failure of the hostage rescue mission in Iran in April, and his inability to negotiate a return of the hostages until after Election Day contributed significantly to his electoral defeat. By contrast Candidate Reagan's promise to inaugurate a new era of unchallengable American power proved an exhilerating prospect to many voters.

Predictably the central theme of the Reagan administration's foreign policy was a clarion call to resist the further expansion of Soviet imperialism. The United States clearly intended to resume its leadership role on the containment front, defined in global terms. High priority was given a prompt U.S. military buildup. A doubling of the percentage increase in the Carter defense budgets for fiscal 1981 and 1982 was proposed by the administration. These increases were partially offset by a three-year program of tax cuts, initiated to stimulate the domestic economy.

In the second year of the Reagan administration the rate of defense spending was further accelerated. For fiscal 1983 a defense budget of $216 billion was proposed in February 1982, an 18 percent increase over the previous year. In a five-year period a total U.S. military expenditure of $1.6 trillion was projected. In outlining the new U.S. military strategy Defense Secretary Caspar W. Weinberger claimed that the proposed increases in defense spending would enable the U.S. to wage "multiple wars across the globe against the forces of the Soviet military empire."(83) The U.S. would be prepared, he said, to launch counter attacks "in places where the Soviets might be more vulnerable" rather than at the initial points of Soviet aggression. Representing a shift away from previous emphasis on U.S. land forces and the requirements of the European theater, the new strategy stressed the overriding importance of radically improving the RDF's air and sealift capabilities. The U.S. would now seek "maritime supremacy" rather than mere parity with the Soviet Navy.

The unilateral steps taken to restore U.S. military strength were complemented by the administration's new arms transfer policy. Even more than in past administrations arms sales would be forcefully used as a key instrument of foreign policy. The alleged mistake of the Carter administration in substituting "theology for a healthy sense of self-preservation" would not, it was

claimed, be repeated under President Reagan.(84)
Far less attention, if any, would be given to the
human rights record of prospective recipients. The
emphasis would be less on restraints to reduce the
level of arms sales and more on their utility in
meeting the Soviet global challenge. Specific
guidelines for arms transfers introduced by the
Carter administration were replaced by more general principles, to be flexibly applied. The relevant questions under the Reagan policy would be
whether the proposed transfer would "promote" mutual interests in countering externally supported
aggression," or whether "any detrimental effects
of the transfer are more than counterbalanced by
positive contributions to United States interests
and objectives."(85)

Under the new policy the previous annual ceiling on arms sales was dropped. American embassies
abroad were encouraged to assist representatives
of U.S. companies producing weapons in marketing
their products. Processing of overseas arms sales
would now be a matter of days rather than weeks.
The application of the new policy to Pakistan and
Saudi Arabia will be considered in separate sections below.


*Secretary Haig's "Strategic Consensus" Formula*

In the 1950s Secretary of State John Foster
Dulles had devised the "northern tier" concept as
the basis for U.S. regional security arrangements
to check Soviet expansion in the Middle East. Turkey, Iran, Iraq, and Pakistan were regional members of the ill-fated Baghdad Pact, later known as
CENTO. By 1979 this U.S.-supported regional grouping was defunct.

To fit the changed circumstances of the 1980s
marked by diminished American power, Secretary of

State Alexander Haig advanced a loosely formulated
concept of "strategic consensus." Baathist Iraq
and Iran's Islamic Republic were obviously not
prospective members of a new regional security effort organized in Washington. The U.S. would have
to rely primarily on its relations with a "southern tier" of Middle Eastern states--Israel, Egypt,
Jordan, Saudi Arabia, and Oman, possibly linked in
some way to Turkey and Pakistan. In Haig's view a
"strategic consensus" upheld by this diverse grouping would be firmly based on shared perceptions of
Soviet expansionism, now sharpened by the recent
Soviet invasion of Afghanistan. Faced with the
danger of future acts of Soviet aggression, these
states would presumably be enabled to transcend
their acknowledged differences.

Secretary Haig's calculations proved faulty.
Virtually no consensus was found to exist among
these seven states. To most Arab states Israel
not the Soviet Union was the primary threat to
regional security. Arab states including Saudi
Arabia which had collectively ejected Egypt from
the Arab League after Sadat made separate peace
with Israel in 1979 were unlikely to join Egypt
in a new grouping under U.S. auspices. Pakistan
was preoccupied with certain problems arising from
its proximity to India. Turkey was not readily
accepted in the Arab world, and was in any case
locked in a bitter dispute with Greece over Cyprus.
Among the Gulf sheikdoms the expansionist drive of
Shia fundamentalism under Iran's impetus was perceived as a greater immediate threat than a Soviet
take-over.

Only in Israel did Secretary Haig meet a positive response. In the Reagan administration Israel
due to its geopolitical position, its efficient
military machine, and its commitment to parliamen-
tary democracy was regarded as a strategic "asset"
that the U.S. should more actively exploit. Is-

rael's government headed by Prime Minister Menachem Begin expressly favored a comprehensive military arrangement with Washington. But in ensuing months intermittent U.S.-Israeli negotiations to set up even a minimal bilateral base for a larger "strategic consensus" were repeatedly interrupted, when Israel took certain actions that aroused protests in Washington—like the Israeli bombing of Iraq's nuclear reactor in June 1981 and Israeli incursions in Lebanon.

As Secretary Haig made little headway in forming an anti-Soviet regional coalition based on an elusive "strategic consensus," the administration was driven more and more to the alternative of strengthening its bilateral relations with regional states. In this process the U.S. increasingly appeared to regard Saudi Arabia as the primary instrument of its Gulf policy.

*The AWACS Sale*

One of the early policy decisions of the Reagan administration was to act on a Saudi arms request which it had inherited from the Carter administration. In 1978 Congress had approved by a narrow margin the White House request for selling 60 F-15s to Saudi Arabia. The Carter administration had assured Congress then that the range and firepower of the F-15s would not be increased. After the Soviet invasion of Afghanistan reactivated regional tensions the Saudis submitted a new arms request to Washington. This included multiple bomb ejection racks to increase the number of bombs that the F-15s could carry, "super-sidewinder" air-to-air missiles, and KC tanker planes to allow refueling of the F-15s. Congressional reaction was sharp. In a letter to President Carter July 8, 1980, 68 senators asked that the request be rejected. The senators argued that sending Saudi Arabia additional military equipment that "would enhance the offensive capability" of the F-15s was not consistent with the "assurances and understandings" given Congress.(86) With a presidential election in the offing the Carter administration decided to delay the Saudi request.

In April 1981 the Reagan administration disclosed that it was planning to seek Congressional approval not only for the additional equipment for the F-15s but also for sale of five AWACS planes. The total cost of the AWACS planes, to be deployed in 1985, was estimated at $5.8 billion. The four U.S. Air Force AWACS planes that had been sent to Saudi Arabia following the outbreak of the Iran-Iraq war in October 1980 were to remain there until the new AWACS were delivered. The administration's announcement set off an uproar in Washington which continued for six months. The pattern of the reaction to the 1978 arms sale was repeated: the activation of the powerful pro-Israel lobby; the counter-activity of professional lobbyists employed by the Saudis; the heated debates in Congress, especially the Senate; the profer of certain concessions by an embattled administration; and a final narrow vote in the Senate favoring the White House.

In its Congressional strategy the administration made an important tactical error. It delayed the formal submission of the Saudi request until September, which allowed Congressional opponents of the sale a long lead-time in mobilizing their followers. In the Senate Senator Bob Packwood played an especially important role in organizing opposition to the Saudi arms sale. Before the Senate hearings began Senator Packwood released the names of 50 Senators--18 of whom were members of the President's own party, who said they opposed the sale.

The opposition presented a number of arguments to support its case. The most important one was its claim that the proposed sale would in fact constitute a serious threat to Israeli security. The 60 high-performance F-15s operating in conjunction with the five AWACS would together represent a formidably integrated air combat team for possible use in a future Arab-Israeli war. Nor would Saudi security itself be advanced due to the likelihood of an Israeli preemptive strike, once the Saudis had acquired such advanced weapons. The opponents argued that continued use of the U.S. AWACS already in Saudi Arabia and under American command was a less risky U.S. indicator of support. They held that the administration had made no real effort to persuade the Saudis to set up a joint command, and pointed out that the administration's gambit of using the arms sale to induce the Saudis to approve a permanent U.S. military base had not worked.

The administration and its supporters responded with counter-arguments.(87) They asserted the AWACS planes were needed to provide the Saudis with a credible air defense for the vitally important oil fields in the eastern provinces. With an AWACS plane on station over the area, fighter planes would have enough time to scramble and challenge low-flying fighter-bombers approaching from across or down the Persian Gulf. The Iran-Iraqi war had underscored the Saudi's need for such advanced equipment. The U.S. would also benefit from the shared intelligence data acquired by these AWACS planes.

The administration pointed out that the present mission of U.S. AWACS had already led to a prepositioning of certain U.S. parts and equipment, which would be accelerated under the Saudi AWACS and F-15s, and that these stores would prove useful to the U.S. in a future Gulf crisis. Finally it was stated that completing the sale would en-

courage the Saudi government to be more cooperative in continued U.S. efforts to expand the
Egyptian-Israeli peace treaty.

A special feature of the prolonged Congressional debate was that Israeli Prime Minister Begin in a visit to Washington personally lobbied
against the AWACS sale. In a news conference October 1 President Reagan made the acerbic comment
that "it is not the business of other nations to
make American foreign policy."(88) Reagan said he
wanted to avoid a perception that the U.S. "was being unduly influenced one way or the other with regard to foreign policy."

Regarded as helpful to the administration's
cause were certain restrictions on the use of the
AWACS which had been negotiated with the Saudi
government.(89) These included the following:
(1)no AWACS flights outside Saudi Arabia's borders
would be permitted without prior U.S. consent;
(2)third country modifications to AWACS equipment
would be prohibited, and no third country personnel would be allowed to perform AWACS maintenance;
(3)a detailed plan to insure the security of AWACS
technology and equipment, a matter of great concern to many Congressmen who feared the AWACS
planes might fall into hands hostile to the U.S.;
(4)an assurance that AWACS intelligence shared
with the U.S. would not be transmitted to third
parties.

Just at the time of the Senate vote the President sent a special letter to Majority Leader Senator Howard Baker stating that prior to the transfer of the AWACS in 1985, he would "certify" to the
Senate that he had obtained agreement with the Saudi government to prevent the possible use of the
aircraft against Israel. The final Senate vote
was 52-48 against the resolution barring the arms
sale to the Saudis. It was widely believed that
the President's willingness to put his personal

prestige at stake as chief articulator of U.S.
foreign policy was the decisive factor in his
winning a close vote. As in 1978 the gains for
the administration were seen as limited. Israel
continued to regard the AWACS sale as a serious
blow to its future security. The Saudis in turn
were disgruntled by the concessions which Congressional criticism had elicited.

In the course of the Senate debate President
Reagan made a statement regarding the U.S. commitment to Saudi Arabia which had potentially high
significance.(90)  His remark was apparently intended to counter the argument that advanced American weapons might fall into enemy hands after a
Saudi revolution. The President said that "Saudi
Arabia we will not permit to be an Iran." Would
then the U.S. intervene militarily to sustain the
position of the royal family in Saudi Arabia?
Some observers insisted that Reagan's statement
in effect extended the Carter Doctrine to include
U.S. responses to internal threats or external
attacks on established pro-Western regions in the
Gulf.

*Aid to Pakistan*

For the Carter administration relations with
Pakistan had been particularly frustrating. Prior
to 1980 the U.S. had attempted to use its foreign
assistance program as leverage to induce Pakistan
to reconsider its nuclear development plans and
correct its alleged violations of human rights.
After 1980 the U.S. sought to reestablish friendly
relations with Pakistan and insure Pakistani cooperation in opposing further Soviet advances in
Southwest Asia.  As cited above Pakistan rejected
the U.S. proposal of $400 million in military and
economic assistance as insufficient.

The Reagan administration, less inhibited by

moralistic goals in its approach to Pakistan, decided to up the ante. In June 1981 the U.S. reached agreement with Pakistan on a substantially larger U.S. aid package.(91) Over the next five years the U.S. would provide Pakistan with $3.2 billion in assistance, half in economic aid and half in military credits. In addition the U.S. agreed to sell Pakistan 40 advanced F-16 fighter aircraft for cash at a total cost of approximately $1.1 billion. Saudi Arabia was expected to supply part of the funds for the F-16 purchases.

Congressional opponents advanced several arguments against the Reagan proposal. The administration had not been able, they said, to persuade Pakistan to adopt appropriate safeguards against future manufacture of nuclear weapons. Some critics maintained that despite the infusion of U.S. high technology, Pakistan still could not defend itself against the Soviet Union. The F-16 aircraft were too advanced for use by the Pakistanis, and in any case were needed by U.S. and NATO forces. Sending advanced weapons to the Pakistanis would only make President Zia's repressive regime more so. Some Congressmen feared that Pakistan would use U.S. arms against India rather than the Soviet Union, confirming India's worst suspicions.

Administration spokesmen responded that the U.S. could scarcely extract concessions from sovereign Pakistan, especially considering the Zia government's ties to the non-alignment movement. They contended that large-scale aid in conventional weapons could give the Pakistanis a greater sense of security and hence make them less likely to take the nuclear option. Pakistan understood, they said, that a nuclear explosion would lead to suspension of the U.S. aid program. In any case the administration attached overriding importance to gaining Pakistan's adherence to an anti-Soviet containment front. In passing the aid package to

Pakistan in December 1981, Congress gave the President the right to waive the Symington amendment to
the Foreign Assistance Act, which barred aid to
countries supposedly engaged in developing nuclear
weapons.

It remains an open question whether resumption
of the U.S. role as a major military supplier to
Pakistan will net the U.S. the anticipated pay-off.
The U.S. relies on Pakistan for continued support
of the principle of Soviet withdrawal from Afghanistan and non-recognition of the Karmal regime. But
Pakistan has continued to have diplomatic discus-
sions with the Russians regarding Soviet troops in
Afghanistan, and maintain economic ties with the
Soviets.  One positive development from Washington's
standpoint was Pakistan's offer of a mutual no-war
pact with India and India's later counter proposal
of a friendship treaty with Pakistan.  If an Indian-
Pakistani detente materialized the U.S. hoped President Zia would give increased attention to his northern border.


*The Israeli Factor*


Like its predecessors the Reagan administration was confronted with the formidable problem
of winning the confidence and support of pro-
Western Arab states in the Gulf without under-
mining the long-standing U.S. commitment to Israel.
Could the administration's high-priority goals of
establishing a strategic consensus against the
Soviets and maintaining the Western oil flow from
the Gulf be reconciled with even qualified support
for the Begin government's vision of an expanded
*Eretz Israel*?  When Reagan entered the White House
he was considered the most pro-Israel President
since 1948.  Yet his administration has been marked
by a series of acrimonious disputes with Israel.

Since they impinge on U.S. policy in the Persian Gulf several aspects of these recurrent frictions will be briefly treated here.

In the early months of the Reagan administration Washington was increasingly perturbed by the Begin government's aggressive policy of supporting additional Jewish settlements in the occupied West Bank. The State Department reiterated the established U.S. position that these settlements were illegal under international law. The administration also criticized Israel's bombing of an Iraqi nuclear reactor near Baghdad in June 1981, in which Israeli aircraft flew across Saudi Arabia. Rejecting Israel's claim that the raid was a legitimate act of self-defense, the U.S. denounced it, voted in favor of a U.N. Security Council resolution condemning Israel and temporarily suspended a U.S. shipment of F-16s to Israel. Washington was similarly distressed by the later Israeli air raid on Beirut directed at PLO headquarters there but killing over 300 Lebanese civilians.

The ongoing crisis in Lebanon became acute in the summer of 1981 when Syria, whose troops had been serving as a peace-keeping force there in the aftermath of the Lebanese civil war, decided to bring in surface-to-air missiles for possible use against Israeli planes which were flying frequent missions over Lebanon. Prime Minister Begin warned that if Syria failed to remove the missiles, Israel would promptly destroy them. President Reagan's special emissary, veteran diplomat Philip Habib, was able after an anxious period to arrange a Lebanese cease-fire. Since neither the U.S. nor Israel had contacts with the PLO, the success of Habib's mission was heavily dependent on supportive mediatory efforts by Saudi Arabia and the United Nations.

In August 1981 Egyptian President Sadat visited Washington followed by Prime Minister Begin, and it was agreed by the three interested parties without evident show of enthusiasm that the long stalemated Egyptian-Israeli autonomy talks on the future status of the occupied territories would shortly resume. The assassination of Sadat, long identified with the Camp David peace process, which occurred on October 1, introduced an unexpected destabilizing factor. Until Sadat's successor, Hosni Mubarak, established firm political control in Egypt, little progress in the autonomy talks was expected. There remained the likelihood that Mubarak would restore Egyptian relations with Arab states.

The espousal of a new Middle Eastern "peace plan" by Crown Prince Fahd of Saudi Arabia in August exposed the thinness of the Reagan administration's commitment to Camp David and created new tensions between the U.S. and Israel. Prince Fahd's plan appeared to be a gloss on U.N. Resolution 242 with the addition of a specific demand for a Palestinian state. It called for Israeli withdrawal from all occupied territories, the right of Palestinians to repatriation, a temporary U.N. trusteeship over the West Bank and Gaza, dismantling the Jewish settlements there, and establishment of a Palestinian state with East Jerusalem as its capital.(92) Its most discussed provision asserted that all states in the area--Israel was not specifically mentioned, had the right to live in peace. Did this presage the long-deferred recognition of Israel by Arab states? If so, could it lead to a breakthrough in the settlement of the Palestinian question? President Reagan and other high U.S. officials called the Fahd plan an "encouraging" development. In Israel Begin denounced it as a plan for the gradual liquidation of Israel and was greatly vexed by Washington's apparent receptivity. The State Department hastily reassured Israel that the U.S. remained firmly committed to Camp David. In the Arab camp the so-called "rejectionist" states like Syria and Iraq were hostile to the Fahd plan. At an important Arab League summit in Fez, Morocco in late November the Fahd proposal failed to win an endorsement.

In an attempt to patch up its fractured relations with Israel the U.S. agreed in late November to put their earlier desultory talks on strategic cooperation in the form of a written agreement. Its provisions fell short of Israeli expectations. They included the exchange of intelligence data, already in effect; stockpiling of U.S. medical supplies in Israel for emergency use as in the case of war in the Gulf; and joint naval exercises. In the Arab world the U.S.-Israeli strategic agreement was viewed not as an anti-Soviet measure but as a grim reminder of massive U.S. support for Israel in the 1973 war. To most Arabs the prospect of Israeli participation in a future collective defense of the Saudi oil fields appeared incongruous.

Suddenly in December 1981 a new crisis in U.S. Israeli relations erupted when the Begin government rushed through the Israeli Knesset legislation extending Israeli civil law to the occupied Golan Heights on the Syrian border, tantamount to annexation by Israel. The Reagan administration's reaction was harsh. The U.S., claiming the new Israeli law violated U.N. Resolution 242 on the occupied territories, supported an unanimous resolution passed by the U.N. Security Council, which declared the Israeli action legally null and void. More serious was the U.S. decision to suspend the recent U.S.-Israeli agreement on strategic cooperation. Resorting to bitter and insulting language, Begin charged the U.S. was attempting to "punish" Israel. In his view the U.S. had in effect cancelled the agreement on strategic cooperation. As the latest crisis subsided attempts were made to resurrect the agreement. Many observers concluded that Haig's ambitious concept of a Middle Eastern "strategic consensus" had been dealt a heavy, if not fatal blow.

*The Question of Continuities*

When new Presidents assume office they frequently stress the innovative elements of their own foreign policy over that of their defeated predecessors. Such was the case with President Reagan in 1981 in regard to the policy he intended to follow in the Persian Gulf. Massive increases in defense expenditures would restore American military power and political influence, which in the Gulf region would be utilized to check further advances of the Soviet juggernaut. The appropriate litmus test for every major U.S. policy in the Gulf would be whether or not it advanced American interests and helped defeat Soviet objectives. Permanent U.S. bases in the Gulf would be more actively sought to insure the effective projection of U.S. military power overseas. The rudimentary RDF machinery inherited from the Carter administration would be substantially amplified and given a unified command structure. Yet despite the sharper tone of the Reagan administration's anti-Soviet rhetoric continuities between Carter's policies in 1978-80 and Reagan's over the last year and a half clearly prevail over the relatively few differences. The latter reflect mainly quantitative differentials rather than qualitative differences.

Both administrations drew the same inference from the Soviet invasion of Afghanistan that it betokened larger Soviet ambitions in the Gulf and the Indian Ocean regions. Both accepted the premise that the direct application of U.S. military power in the Gulf was the only feasible U.S. al-

ternative after the fall of the Shah in Iran. Both
assumed that bilateral security arrangements with
Gulf states were supplemental to the unilateral
exercise of U.S. military power. Both schemed for
U.S. regional bases and settled for less.

In the strategic calculations of both administrations Saudi Arabia is assigned a central
place. Considering its geopolitical position, its
rich oil resources, the marked dependency of its
armed forces on U.S. weapons and military training, and the pro-Western outlook of the Saudi
royal family, Saudi Arabia has no near rival in
the Gulf as the object of U.S. preferential treat-
ment. Both Carter and Reagan proved willing to
incur the wrath of the powerful pro-Israel lobby
in Congress by promoting the delivery of advanced
U.S. aircraft to the Saudis. In both the 1978
F-15 sale and the 1981 AWACS sale the validity and
strength of the U.S. commitment to Saudi Arabia
was believed to be at stake and deserving of unwavering support. In 1981 President Reagan went
so far as to underwrite the political future of
the Saudi royal family, although it remains to be
seen whether his supportive statement was simply
a tactical ploy to facilitate Senate acceptance of
the AWACS sale.

Admittedly the official arms transfer policy
of the two administrations is differently formulated. The Reagan administration places virtually
no restrictions on sales of U.S. conventional weapons abroad, and large quantitative increases have
been undertaken. But in practice the stricter policy of the Carter administration was flexibly applied, especially in continued heavy arms sales to
the Shah and in the hastily arranged arms shipment
to North Yemen in 1979.

Both administrations have manifested a certain
ambivalence in the conduct of relations with Israel.
Both Carter and Reagan have castigated Israel's in-

cursions into Lebanon, but each has drawn back from imposing effective long-term sanctions against Israel. Both administrations sponsored the sale of advanced weapons to Saudi Arabia which invariably provokes a critical outcry in Jerusalem. In similar situations both administrations resorted to damage control by reassuring Israel the U.S. would act to maintain Israel's continued military superiority over its Arab neighbors.

Some Reagan critics charge his administration with paying only lip service to the Egyptian-Israeli autonomy talks and failing to advance constructive U.S. proposals for the early resolution of the Palestinian question. But after the seizure of U.S. hostages in Iran in 1979 the Carter administration gave steadily decreasing attention to keeping the autonomy talks on track, and by late 1980 many observers held that the Camp David peace process, initiated by Carter, had reached a dead end.

Both administrations have been afflicted with bureaucratic factionalism adversely affecting the coherence of their respective policies in the Middle East. In the Carter administration Secretary Vance and Presidential adviser Brzezinski had serious differences as cited above over U.S. policy in Iran and the use of force to advance U.S. regional goals. In the Reagan administration the rivalry between Secretary Haig and Defense Secretary Weinberger--up to Haig's departure in July 1982, had repercussions in the Middle East. Weinberger was widely regarded as more pro-Arab and less supportive of Israel than Haig. Weinberger actively pushed for a closer U.S. military relationship with Saudi Arabia and for using expanded U.S. arms sales to prevent Arab defections to the Soviet camp. Haig reportedly used his influence in several instances to modulate negative U.S. reactions to aggressive acts by the Begin government,

cautioning the White House against publicly airing
U.S.-Israeli differences. Weinberger advocated
punitive action by the U.S. in response to what
were regarded as aggressive actions by Israel. In
the one case Carter's indecisiveness fed the chronic differences among his advisers, in the other
Reagan's preoccupation with domestic policy and
his markedly lesser interest in foreign policy
questions allowed factional differences on foreign policy to fester.


*Final Comments*

Thus far the Reagan administration's Gulf
policy has netted slight gains. Secretary Haig's
efforts to organize a wide-ranging "strategic
consensus" against the Soviet Union were not pro-
ductive. The administration's obsessive anti-
Sovietism ran counter to the region's own preoc-
cupations: how OPEC will handle the oil "glut,"
fears of further inroads by Islamic fundamentalists, a new acute phase in the unresolved Palestine question. Washington's search for U.S.
regional military bases has not proved rewarding.
With the exception of Oman the pro-Western Arab
states in the Gulf will countenance U.S. forces
only "over the horizon." Whether they will be
granted wider access in a future Gulf crisis de-
pends very much on the actual circumstances at
that time. Significant arms deals have been made
with Saudi Arabia and Pakistan, but the U.S. has
only limited control over future use of this weaponry.
    Two recent events in the Gulf underscore the
tenuousness and narrow scope of the American position. In 1981 a six-nation Gulf Cooperation Coun-
cil(GCC) under Saudi leadership was formed to promote political and economic cooperation among its

members, and in early 1982 the GCC established a joint command for its combined military forces. So far as is known the U.S. played no role in the formation of the GCC, nor does it have direct links with its headquarters in Riyadh.

In late 1981 an RDF exercise called "Operation Bright Star" included Egypt, the Sudan, Somalia, and Oman. British and French personnel were marginally involved. The size of the participating units was beefed up after Sadat's assassination seemed to require a more impressive display of American military power. The relevant point here is that Oman placed severe restrictions on the RDF unit deployed there. The U.S. Marine landing force was allowed to penetrate only four miles on the Arabian Sea coast and remain on Omani territory for only 30 hours.

At this writing in July 1982 the U.S. is confronted with two regional developments of great importance. The first is the apparent military victory of Iran's Islamic Republic in its prolonged war with Iraq. It is as yet uncertain whether Iranian forces will cross into Iraq in order to insure the overthrow of Saddam Hussein, whom the Iranians regard as the instigator of the war. A new expansionist phase by Islamic militants is now predicted for the Gulf region with incalculable consequences for U.S. policy. Meanwhile the U.S. maintains a stance of "watchful waiting" as the Iran-Iraqi war winds down, virtually powerless to influence the course of events. If repetitions of the 1981 coup in Bahrain occur, it is uncertain what the U.S. response, if any, will be.

Israel's invasion of Lebanon in June to secure the military and political liquidation of the PLO organization promises to usher in a new era in the Arab-Israeli conflict. At this writing it is not known whether the proposed U.S. naval mission to remove the PLO from West Beirut will in fact be employed. The critical question is whether Israel will attempt to follow up its military victory in Lebanon with a policy of outright annexation of the West Bank and Gaza territories, or whether the U.S. will utilize its acknowledged but seldom used leverage to induce Israel to accept a genuine system of Palestinian autonomy under the terms of Camp David. Washington's anticipated reabsorption in the stalemated autonomy negotiations will deflect attention away from the presently highly unstable situation in the Persian Gulf. The outlines of U.S. policy in the Gulf in the last half of the Reagan administration are presently indiscernible. Lacking a conceptually fixed regional focus the Reagan policy is likely to continue to have a reactive, improvised character.

- - -

In reviewing the past turbulent decade in the Persian Gulf certain images stand out: the last British warship leaving Aden harbor as the decade began; the arrival of President Nixon and Secretary Kissinger on Air Force One in Teheran in May 1972, to open up the spigot of U.S. arms shipments to the Shah; the long lines at U.S. gas stations following the imposition of the OAPEC oil embargo in 1973-74; the still-crated U.S. weapons on loading docks in Sana after the abruptly cancelled Yemeni war in 1979; the public squares in Teheran filled with irate masses during the hostage crisis, shaking televised fists at the "Great Satan;" the U.S. helicopters stranded in the Iranian desert in the abortive rescue mission; Israeli planes of U.S. origin flying over Saudi air space to bomb the Iraqi nuclear reactor in 1981; U.S. guns supplied to the Shah used by Khomeini's forces in winning

the war with Iraq; the U.S. Marines' abbreviated
landing for testing purposes on the Omani coast at
the end of the decade.   John Campbell's telling
phrase to describe regional policy sticks in the
mind: "a house of containment built on shifting
sands."

July 1982

## Notes

(1)  Arab nationalists reject the "Persian" modifier and substitute the "Arabian" referent.  The conventional Western usage of "Persian" is followed in this report.

(2)  The U.S. currently imports between 25-30 percent of its oil imports from the Persian Gulf, Western Europe 57 percent, Japan 70 percent.

(3)  Beginning in 1820 the British entered into a series of special treaties with the Gulf sheikdoms which gave them control of foreign affairs and defense.  These were replaced by treaties of friendship in 1971.

(4)  The Twelver Shias believe in the total submission to an infallible spiritual leader known as an Imam.  The 12th Imam mysteriously disappeared

in the 9th century, and his reappearance is awaited by his followers.

(5)  *The Middle East: U.S. Policy, Israel, Oil and the Arabs*, Congressional Quarterly, 4th edition, 1979, p. 154.

(6)  *The Middle East*, Congressional Quarterly, 5th edition, 1981, p. 188.

(7)  *The Persian Gulf and the Strait of Hormuz*, R. K. Ramazani, Sijthoff and Noordhoff, 1979, p. 42.

(8)  Harvard University professor of government, Stanley Hoffman, is a leading spokesman of this second school.

(9)  "Moscow and the Persian Gulf," David L. Price, *Problems of Communism*, April, 1979, p. 7.

(10)  Ramazani, pp. 51-2.

(11)  *The Foreign Relations of Iran: A Developing State in a Zone of Great-Power Conflict*, Shahram Chubin and Sepehr Zabih, University of California Press, 1974, pp. 80-1.

(12)  Ibid., p. 257.

(13)  "U.S. Foreign Policy for the 1970's: Building for Peace," *A Report to the Congress* by President Richard M. Nixon, 1971, pp. 12-14.

(14)  House Committee on Foreign Affairs, *New Perspectives on the Persian Gulf*, 1973, pp. 7-8.

(15)  Ibid., p. 39.

(16)   Text of Statement, *Keesing's Contemporary Archives*, 1972, pp. 25313-4.

(17)   *Paved With Good Intenions: The American Experience and Iran*, Barry Rubin, Oxford Press, 1980, p. 102.

(18)   Ibid., p.116.

(19)   *White House Years*, Henry Kissinger, Little Brown & Co., 1979, p. 1264.

(20)   House Committee on International Relations, *U.S. Arms Policies in the Persian Gulf: Past, Present, and Future*, 1979, p. 135. (Hereafter referred to as *PGArms*)

(21)   Ibid., p. 135.

(22)   *The Global Politics of Arms Sales*, Andrew J. Pierre, Council of Foreign Relations, 1982, pp. 148-49.

(23)   Ibid., p. 149.

(24)   *PGArms*, p. 139.   Some estimates were as high as 40,000 Americans in Iran at this period.

(25)   *The New York Times*, February 20, 1975.

(26)   *The Illusion of Peace: Foreign Policy in the Nixon Years*, Tad Szulc, The Viking Press, 1978, p. 585.

(27)   Kissinger, p. 1265.

(28)   Later PFLOAG dropped "Arabian Gulf" from its acronym.

(29) *Debacle: The American Failure in Iran*, Michael Ledeen and William Lewis, Knopf, 1981, p. 55.

(30) Rubin, p. 155.

(31) The original concession of the Standard Oil Co. of California in 1933 covered 360,000 square miles and was later enlarged by an additional 80,000 square miles. Later Texaco, Exxon, and Mobil bought into ARAMCO.

(32) *Search for Security: Saudi Arabian Oil and American Foreign Policy, 1939-1949*, Aaron David Miller, Chapel Hill, 1980, p. 130.

(33) Ibid., p. 145. Forrestal's statement to Secretary of State James F. Byrnes, August 1, 1945.

(34) *Saudi Arabia and Oil Diplomacy*, Sheikh Rustum Ali, Praeger, 1976, p. 105.

(35) *PGArms*, p. 27.

(36) *Saudi Arabia in the 1980s: Foreign Policy, Security, and Oil*, William B. Quandt, The Brookings Institution, 1981, p. 102. Other estimates are of 45,000 soldiers in the Saudi army, 35,000 in the National Guard.

(37) The several consecutive agreements between the U.S. and the Saudi government are summarized in *PGArms*, pp. 30-38.

(38) *The New York Times*, February 20, 1975.

(39) *The Middle East*, Cong/Q, 4th edition, p. 156.

(40) Ibid., p. 83.

(41)  Ibid., p. 84.

(42)  *The Middle East*, Cong/Q, 5th edition, p. 91.

(43)  Ibid., p. 91.

(44)  "Oil: The Issue of American Intervention,"
Robert W. Tucker, *Commentary*, January 1975.

(45)  *Business Week*, January 13, 1975.

(46)  Ramazani, p.62.

(47)  See Richard Haass's essay, "Saudi Arabia and
Iran: the Twin Pillars in Revolutionary Times" in
*The Security of the Persian Gulf*, edited by Hossein
Amirsadeghi, Croom Helm, 1981, pp. 151-169. Haass
stresses the cooperative aspects in the Iran-Saudi
relationship.

(48)  Quandt, p. 129.

(49)  *PGArms*, pp. 104-5.

(50)  Ibid., pp. 90-1.

(51)  Ibid., pp. 10 and 51.  Since the British
Royal Air Force retained a base at Masirah Island
at that time, the announcement was made jointly
by the British and Omani governments.

(52)  Ibid., pp. 76-7.

(53)  The annual reports on the Persian Gulf
issued under the auspices of the House Committee
on Foreign Affairs between 1973-77 provide many
examples of Congressional criticism of administration policy in the Gulf.

(54)  Pierre, p. 49.

(55)  Ibid., p. 49.

(56)  House Committee on International Relations, *Oil Fields as Military Objectives, A Feasibility Study*, 1975.

(57)  Text of President Carter's statement, *American Foreign Relations: A Documentary Record (1977)*, Council of Foreign Relations 1979, pp. 187-9.

(58)  Ledeen and Lewis, pp. 84-5.

(59)  See text of Secretary Vance's address in April 1977, *American Foreign Relations: A Documentary Record*, pp. 165-71.

(60)  Rubin, p. 194.

(61)  Quandt, pp. 112-13.

(62)  See the author's study, *The Camp David Peace Process*, Tompson and Rutter, 1981, pp. 4-18.

(63)  Quandt, p. 120.

(64)  Ledeen and Lewis, p. 124.  Later President Carter publicly criticized the performance of his intelligence officials.

(65)  See Sullivan's *Mission to Iran*, W. W. Norton, 1981, pp. 200-48.  Sullivan complained his superiors frequently ignored his memoranda and cables, leaving him without instructions on important matters.

(66)  Ledeen and Lewis, p. 191.

(67) *Conflict in the Persian Gulf*, Murray Gordon, editor, Facts on File, N.Y., 1981, pp. 123-4. Hereafter referred to as *PG Conflict*.

(68) *Security in the Persian Gulf, No. 4: The Role of Outside Powers*, Shahram Chubin, The International Institute for Strategic Studies, 1982, p. 58.

(69) *PG Conflict*, p. 125.

(70) "The Middle East: A Year of Turmoil," J. C. Hurewitz, *Foreign Affairs*, Spring, 1981, pp. 552-53.

(71) U.S. State Department *Current Policy* No. 132, January 23, 1980, p. 2.

(72) Text of President Truman's speech, March 12, 1948, *Keesing's Contemporary Archives* (1946-48 volume), pp. 8491-2.

(73) Text of President Eisenhower's speech, January 5, 1957, *Keesing's* (1957-58 volume), pp. 15305-6.

(74) *Washington Post*, December 6, 1979.

(75) Senate Committee on Armed Services, *Hearings*, Fiscal 1981 Defense Department appropriations (1980), Part I, p. 441.

(76) *The Rapid Deployment Force*, Jeffrey Record, Institute for Foreign Policy Analysis, 1981, p. 53. Record's report is a cogent presentation of RDF's inadequacies.

(77) Text of Secretary Brown's speech to the Council of Foreign Relations, March 6, 1980, U.S. State Department *Bulletin*, May 1980, p. 65.

(78) Ibid., p. 65. Italics added.

(79) *PG Conflict*, pp. 138-39.

(80) *The New York Times*, February 2, 1980.

(81) *Keesing's Archives*, (1980 volume), pp. 30379, 30596.

(82) *PG Conflict*, pp. 161-2.

(83) *Facts on File*, February 12, 1982, p. 84.

(84) Statement by Undersecretary of State for Security Assistance James L. Buckley, U.S. State Department, *Current Policy* No. 279, May 21, 1981.

(85) Pierre, p. 63.

(86) *The Middle East,* Cong/Q, 5th edition, p. 61.

(87) *The New York Times*, October 1, 1981.

(88) Ibid., October 2, 1981.

(89) Ibid., October 6, 1981.

(90) Ibid., December 16, 1981.

(91) "The Middle East: A House of Containment Built on Shifting Sands," John C. Campbell, *Foreign Affairs*, Spring, 1982, pp. 601-2.

(92) Ibid., pp. 616-17.

SELECTED BIBLIOGRAPHY

*Books*

Ali, Sheikh Rustum. *Saudi Arabia and Oil Diplomacy*. New York: Praeger, 1976.

Amirsadeghi, Hossein, ed. *The Security of the Persian Gulf*. London: Croom Helm, 1981.

Anthony, John Duke. *Arab States of the Lower Gulf: People, Politics, Petroleum*. Washington, D.C.: The Middle East Institute, 1975.

Beazley, Kim C. and Clark, Ian. *The Politics of Intrusion: The Superpowers and the Indian Ocean*. Sydney: Alternative Pub. Cooperative, 1979.

Bezboruah, Monoranian. *U.S. Strategy in the Indian Ocean: The International Response*. New York: Praeger, 1977.

Chubin, Shahram, and Zabih, Sepehr. *The Foreign Relations of Iran: A Developing State in a Zone of Great-Power Conflict*. Berkeley: University of California Press, 1974.

_____. *Security in the Persian Gulf 4: The Role of Outside Powers*. Totowa, N.J.: Allanheld, Osmun & Co., 1982.

Collins, John M. *U.S.-Soviet Military Balance: Concepts and Capabilities 1960-1980*. New York: McGraw-Hill, 1980.

Cottrell, Alvin J., ed. *The Persian Gulf States: A General Survey*. Baltimore: Johns Hopkins University, 1980.

_____, and Bray, Frank. *Military Forces in the Persian Gulf*. Beverley Hills, Calif.: Sage Publications, 1978.

Gordon, Murray. *Conflict in the Persian Gulf*. New York: Facts on File, 1981.

Kissinger, Henry. *White House Years*. Boston: Little, Brown, and Co., 1979.

_____. *Years of Upheaval*. Boston: Little, Brown, and Co., 1982.

Ledeen, Michael, and Lewis, William. *Debacle: The American Failure in Iran*. New York, Alfred A. Knopf, 1981.

Long, David E. *The Persian Gulf: An Introduction to Its People, Politics, and Economics*. Boulder, Colo.: Westview Press, 1976.

Mangold, Peter. *Superpower Interventions in the Middle East*. New York: St. Martin's Press, 1978.

Maull, Hanns. *Oil and Influence: the Oil Weapon Examined*. London: The International Institute for Strategic Studies (Adelphi Papers, No. 117), 1975.

Nakhleh, Emile A. *Arab-American Relations in the Persian Gulf*. Washington, D.C.: American Enterprise Institute for Public Policy Research, 1975.

Niblock, Tim, ed. *Social and Economic Development in the Arab Gulf*. London: Croom Helm, 1980.

Novik, Nimrod, and Starr, Joyce. *Challenges in the Middle East: Regional Dynamics and Western Security*. New York: Praeger, 1981.

Pierre, Andrew J. *The Global Politics of Arms Sales*. Princeton: Princeton University Press, 1982.

Quandt, William B. *Saudi Arabia in the 1980s: Foreign Policy, Security, and Oil*. Washington, D.C.: The Brookings Institution, 1981.

Ramazani, Rouhollah. *The Persian Gulf: Iran's Role*. Charlottesville: University of Virginia, 1972.

_____. *The Persian Gulf and the Strait of Hormuz*. Alphen aan den Rijn: Sijthoff and Noordhoff, 1979.

Record, Jeffrey. *The Rapid Deployment Force and U.S. Military Intervention in the Persian Gulf*. Cambridge, Mass.: Institute for Foreign Policy Analysis, Inc., 1981.

Rubin, Barry. *Paved with Good Intentions: The American Experience and Iran*. New York: Oxford University Press, 1980.

Sullivan, William H. *Mission to Iran*. New York: W.W. Norton, 1981.

Szulc, Tad. *The Illusion of Peace: Foreign Policy in the Nixon Years*. New York: Viking Press, 1978.

Tahtinen, Dale R. *Arms in the Persian Gulf*. Washington, D.C.: American Enterprise Institute, 1974.

*The Middle East*. Washington, D.C.: Congressional Quarterly, 4th edition (1979) and 5th edition (1981).

Yorke, Valerie. *The Gulf in the 1980s*. London: Chatham House Papers No. 6, 1980.

*Government Publications*:

U.S. Congress, House Committee on Foreign Affairs:
    (1) *U.S. Interests and Policy toward the Persian Gulf* (1972)
    (2) *New Perspectives on the Persian Gulf* (1973)
    (3) *The Persian Gulf 1974: Money, Politics, Arms, and Power* (1974)
    (4) *Oil Fields as Military Objectives: A Feasibility Study* (1975)
    (5) *U.S. Arms Policies in the Persian Gulf and Red Sea: Past, Present and Future* (1977)

(6) *U.S. Interests and Policies toward the Persian Gulf* (1980)
(7) *U.S. Security Interests in the Persian Gulf* (1981)
(8) *Saudi Arabia and the U.S.: The New Context in an Evolving Relationship* (1981)

U.S. Congress, Senate Committee on Foreign Relations:
(1) *U.S. Military Sales to Iran* (1976)
(2) *Study Visit to Saudi Arabia* (1979)
(3) *U.S. Security Interests and Policies in Southwest Asia* (1980)
(4) *Arms Sales Package to Saudi Arabia* (1981)

U.S. Congress, Joint Economic Committee:
(1) *U.S. Overseas Projection Forces* (1978)
(2) *The U.S. Role in a Changing World* (1979)
(3) *The Persian Gulf: Are We Committed? At What Cost?* (1981)

U.S. Department of State:
(1) *Bulletin*, monthly
(2) *Current Policy*, occasional statements

*Articles*

Binder, Leonard. "The United States in the Middle East." *Current History*, January 1980.

Campbell, John C. "Middle East: The Burdens of Empire." *Foreign Affairs*, Spring, 1979.

_____. "The House of Containment Built on Shifting Sands." *Foreign Affairs*, Spring, 1982.

Campbell, W. R., and Darvich, Djarchid. "Global Implications of the Islamic Revolution." *Journal of South Asian and Middle East Studies*. Fall, 1981.

Chubin, Shahram. "U.S. Security Interests in the Persian Gulf in the 1980s." *Daedalus*, Fall, 1980.

Dawisha, Adeed I. "Iraq and the Arab World: The Gulf War and After." *World Today*, May, 1981.

Eilts, Hermann F. "Security Considerations in the Persian Gulf." *International Security*, Fall, 1980.

Hollen, Christopher Van. "Don't Engulf the Gulf." *Foreign Affairs*, Summer, 1981.

Holliday, Fred. "The Arc of Crisis and the New Cold War." *Merip Reports*, Oct.-Dec., 1981.

Hurewitz, J. C. "The Middle East: A Year of Turmoil." *Foreign Affairs*, Spring, 1981.

Levy, Walter. "Oil and the Decline of the West." *Foreign Affairs*, Summer, 1980.

Newsom, David D. "America Engulfed." *Foreign Policy*, Summer, 1981.

Price, David Lynn. "Moscow and the Persian Gulf." *Problems of Communism*, April, 1979.

Quandt, William. "The Middle East Crises." *Foreign Affairs*, Spring, 1980.

Ross, Dennis. "Considering Soviet Threats in the Persian Gulf." *International Security*, Fall, 1981.

Rubinstein, Alvin. "The Soviet Presence in the Arab World." *Current History*, October, 1981.

Sullivan, William H. "Dateline Iran: The Road Not Taken." *Foreign Policy*, Fall, 1980.

Tucker, Robert W. "Oil: The Issue of American Involvement." *Commentary*, January, 1975.

_____. "American Power and the Persian Gulf." *Commentary*, November, 1980.

_____. "The Middle East: Carterism without Carter." *Commentary*, September, 1981.